POLAR REGIONS

Human Impacts

OUR FRAGILE PLANET

Atmosphere

Biosphere

Climate

Geosphere

Humans and the Natural Environment

Hydrosphere

Oceans

Polar Regions

POLAR REGIONS

Human Impacts

DANA DESONIE, PH.D.

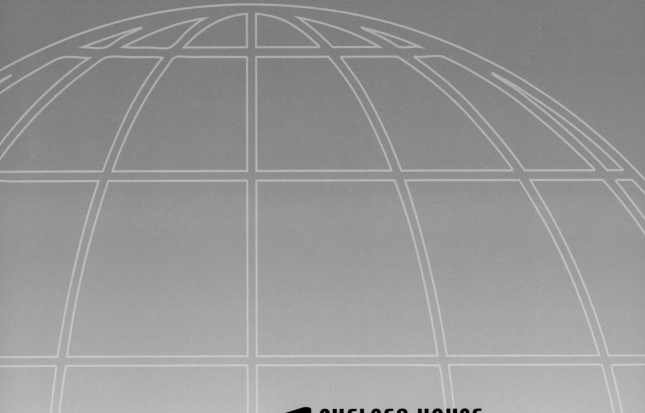

CHELSEA HOUSE
PUBLISHERS
An imprint of Infobase Publishing

Polar Regions

Copyright © 2008 by Dana Desonie, Ph.D.

All rights reserved. No part of this book may be reproduced or utilized in any form or by any means, electronic or mechanical, including photocopying, recording, or by any information storage or retrieval systems, without permission in writing from the publisher. For information contact:

Chelsea House
An imprint of Infobase Publishing
132 West 31st Street
New York, NY 10001

Library of Congress Cataloging-in-Publication Data
Desonie, Dana.
  Polar regions: human impacts / Dana Desonie.
    p. cm. — (Our fragile planet)
  Includes bibliographical references and index.
  ISBN-13: 978-0-8160-6218-8 (hardcover)
  ISBN-10: 0-8160-6218-8 (hardcover)
  1. Ecology—Polar regions—Juvenile literature. 2. Nature—Effect of human beings on—Juvenile literature. 3. Polar regions—Juvenile literature. I. Title. II. Series.

  QH541.5.P6D47 2007
  578.0911—dc22   2007029994

Chelsea House books are available at special discounts when purchased in bulk quantities for businesses, associations, institutions, or sales promotions. Please call our Special Sales Department in New York at (212) 967-8800 or (800) 322-8755.

You can find Chelsea House on the World Wide Web at http://www.chelseahouse.com

Text design by Annie O'Donnell
Cover design by Ben Peterson

Printed in the United States of America

Bang NMSG 10 9 8 7 6 5 4 3 2 1

This book is printed on acid-free paper.

All links and Web addresses were checked and verified to be correct at the time of publication. Because of the dynamic nature of the Web, some addresses and links may have changed since publication and may no longer be valid.

Cover photograph: © Thomas & Pat Leeson/Photo Researchers, Inc.

Contents

Preface

The planet is a marvelous place: a place with blue skies, wild storms, deep lakes, and rich and diverse ecosystems. The tides ebb and flow, baby animals are born in the spring, and tropical rain forests harbor an astonishing array of life. The Earth sustains living things and provides humans with the resources to maintain a bountiful way of life: water, soil, and nutrients to grow food, and the mineral and energy resources to build and fuel modern society, among many other things.

The physical and biological sciences provide an understanding of the whys and hows of natural phenomena and processes—why the sky is blue and how metals form, for example—and insights into how the many parts are interrelated. Climate is a good example. Among the many influences on the Earth's climate are the circulation patterns of the atmosphere and the oceans, the abundance of plant life, the quantity of various gases in the atmosphere, and even the size and shapes of the continents. Clearly, to understand climate it is necessary to have a basic understanding of several scientific fields and to be aware of how these fields are interconnected.

As Earth scientists like to say, the only thing constant about our planet is change. From the ball of dust, gas, and rocks that came together 4.6 billion years ago to the lively and diverse globe that orbits the Sun today, very little about the Earth has remained the same for long. Yet, while change is fundamental, people have altered the environment unlike any other species in Earth's history. Everywhere there are reminders of our presence. A look at the sky might show a sooty cloud or a jet contrail. A look at the sea might reveal plastic refuse, oil, or only a few fish swimming where once they had been countless. The land has been deforested and strip-mined. Rivers and lakes have been polluted. Changing conditions and habitats have caused some plants and animals to expand their populations, while others have become extinct. Even the climate—which for millennia was thought to be beyond human influence—has been shifting due to alterations in the makeup of atmospheric gases brought about by human activities. The planet is changing fast and people are the primary cause.

OUR FRAGILE PLANET is a set of eight books that celebrate the wonders of the world by highlighting the scientific processes behind them. The books also look at the science underlying the tremendous influence humans are having on the environment. The set is divided into volumes based on the large domains on which humans have had an impact: *Atmosphere, Climate, Hydrosphere, Oceans, Geosphere, Biosphere,* and *Polar Regions.* The volume *Humans and the Natural Environment* describes the impact of human activity on the planet and explores ways in which we can live more sustainably.

A core belief expressed in each volume is that to mitigate the impacts humans are having on the Earth, each of us must understand the scientific processes that operate in the natural world. We must understand how human activities disrupt those processes and use that knowledge to predict ways that changes in one system will affect seemingly unrelated systems. These books express the belief that science is the solid ground from which we can reach an agreement on the behavioral changes that we must adopt—both as individuals and as a society—to solve the problems caused by the impact of humans on our fragile planet.

Acknowledgments

I would like to thank, above all, the scientists who have dedicated their lives to the study of the Earth, especially those engaged in the important work of understanding how human activities are impacting the planet. Many thanks to the staff of Facts On File and Chelsea House for their guidance and editing expertise: Frank Darmstadt, Executive Editor; Brian Belval, Senior Editor; and Leigh Ann Cobb, independent developmental editor. Dr. Tobi Zausner located the color images that illustrate our planet's incredible beauty and the harsh reality of the effects human activities are having on it. Thanks also to my agent, Jodie Rhodes, who got me involved in this project.

Family and friends were a great source of support and encouragement as I wrote these books. Special thanks to the May '97 Moms, who provided the virtual water cooler that kept me sane during long days of writing. Cathy Propper was always enthusiastic as I was writing the books, and even more so when they were completed. My mother, Irene Desonie, took great care of me as I wrote for much of June 2006. Mostly importantly, my husband, Miles Orchinik, kept things moving at home when I needed extra writing time and provided love, support, and encouragement when I needed that, too. This book is dedicated to our children, Reed and Maya, who were always loving, and usually patient. I hope these books do a small bit to help people understand how their actions impact the future for all children.

Introduction

The polar regions are unique sites on an exceptional planet. The Arctic and Antarctic regions, which lie remote and distant from the rest of the world, form the ice caps of the Earth. Until recently, these areas were extremely difficult to reach from the more temperate, populated regions of the world. With their cycles of dark and bitter cold winters and long and plentiful summers, the polar areas have existed without much impact from human civilization.

The north and south polar regions go through winter and summer cycles at opposite times of the year, but they both annually experience months of darkness and months of sunlight. During the long summers, plants bloom on land and in the seas. Water remains captured in enormous amounts of ice that takes many forms: sea ice, ice sheets, ice shelves, icebergs, frozen lakes and streams, and snow. Even the ground is frozen much of the year. Polar life is unique, either adapted to these harsh conditions or migrating into the area to partake of the summer bounty. Marine life abounds in the cold seas. Tiny plankton form the base of an ecosystem that includes abundant fish, enormous whales, plentiful seals, and fabulous diving and swimming birds.

Still, the Arctic and Antarctic are very different from each other: The Arctic is an ocean surrounded by land, while the Antarctic is land surrounded by an ocean. Although these two situations may not seem very different, they result in distinct conditions. Both locations are bitter cold and dry in the winter, but the presence of land around the Arctic allows for more variability in temperature and precipitation. Winters and summers in the Arctic are quite a bit warmer than in the

Antarctic. In many northern locations, temperatures hover around the freezing point of water for a portion of the year. Because ice collects better over frigid land than over relatively warm seawater, the ice sheet that has grown over Antarctica far exceeds in area and volume the sea ice that spreads over the Arctic Ocean. The Arctic has an ice sheet, too; but the Greenland ice sheet is much smaller than the one that covers Antarctica.

Arctic and Antarctic plant and animal species are also dissimilar. Each location has relatively few different species when compared with the species diversity found in more temperate climates. This is because few species have been able to adapt to the severe conditions at the poles. Polar region species are unusual. Herds of large mammals migrate through the lands that surround the Arctic sea in summer; but, in Antarctica, the only large mammals were introduced by human visitors in the years between about A.D. 900 to about 1300. Polar bears and walrus hunt from ice floes in the Arctic, but penguins are the main animals that live in the Antarctic. Marine creatures in both regions are similar: Large whales, seals, fish, and birds take advantage of the productive seas, and some large marine mammals make the long annual journey from one polar region to the other to reap the summertime abundance.

Human habitation and resource exploitation have had very different impacts in the two locations. While about 4 million people currently reside in the Arctic, only about 4,000 scientists inhabit Antarctica. The Arctic has a long history of habitation by native people who developed a complex set of rituals and skills to survive in the unforgiving conditions. Their well-timed practices took advantage of seasonal rhythms that allowed them to thrive, or at least survive, year round. There is no evidence that native people ever lived in the Antarctic—hence, human beings have not had as great an impact on its environment.

When the inhabitants of the temperate zones think of the polar regions, they typically think of clean, white, and pristine lands. Compared with the rest of the world, which has been greatly modified by human activities, they mostly are. Relatively little pollution is produced in the polar areas, and what little pollution is there, comes from far-away places. The exploitation of the Arctic for oil and minerals results in some pollution. However, Antarctica, with its land buried beneath a thick layer of ice, is largely off limits to commercial interests.

Pollution in the polar regions largely travels in from elsewhere. Compared with the Arctic region, the Antarctic is isolated from many of the environmental problems of the rest of the world. For one thing, currents that circulate through the main portions of the ocean basins do not reach that far south. The land that drains into the surrounding ocean is cloaked in ice and uninhabited. Little land exists north of the Antarctic seas because of the way most of the continents' land masses narrow at their southernmost reaches. The environmental problems that the Antarctic does experience are largely caused by the emissions of pollutants into the atmosphere from far away. Due to conditions that are particular to the Antarctic, the ozone hole is centered there. The worldwide problem of global warming is being felt there, too. Nor is the Southern Ocean surrounding Antarctica immune to the problems of overfishing and overhunting that plague the world's oceans overall: Over the past few centuries, Antartica's marine creatures have been subject to both.

The situation in the Arctic is vastly different from the Antarctic. Because 70% of the world's land, including the most developed regions on Earth, is located in the Northern Hemisphere, the Arctic is vulnerable to the environmental problems that plague those lands. Pollutants travel in by air and via ocean currents and across lands in rivers that drain into the region. As a result, Arctic animals have surprisingly large concentrations of some toxic chemicals in their tissues and body fat. The conditions that cause Arctic temperatures to be more variable also keep air from becoming as stagnant as in Antarctica. For this reason, ozone depletion in the Arctic is much less of a problem than in the Antarctic. Like the Antarctic, though, the Arctic is warming at a higher rate than the rest of the planet, and the effects of global warming are being felt more strongly there. Overfishing and overhunting are also a concern.

This volume of OUR FRAGILE PLANET explores the polar regions and how they are uniquely affected by environmental problems. Because their harsh conditions make them more vulnerable to some environmental ills, particularly global warming, the polar regions have been called the "canary in the coal mine." (This expression refers to the time before monitoring devices were invented to detect dangerous gases in mines. To serve as a warning, coal miners kept caged canaries in the mines with them. Because the birds were more sensitive to deadly fumes than the miners, the miners knew that when the birds died it was time to get out of the mine.) The changes now being seen in the polar regions, especially in the Arctic, may also be a forewarning of large changes to take place on the rest of the Earth.

Part One of this volume details the physical, chemical, and biological characteristics of the two polar areas. Part Two describes the problems—particularly global warming—caused by atmospheric pollutants, with an emphasis on the Arctic and the ozone hole in the Antarctic. Due to its proximity to the developed parts of the world, chemical pollution is much more serious a problem in the Arctic, which is the focus of Part Three. Part Four describes overfishing and overhunting in the Arctic and Southern Oceans. Finally, Part Five looks at the protections that are already in place for the Arctic and Antarctic and imagines the future of the Arctic—a future that may arrive sooner than most people realize.

PART ONE

THE POLAR REGIONS

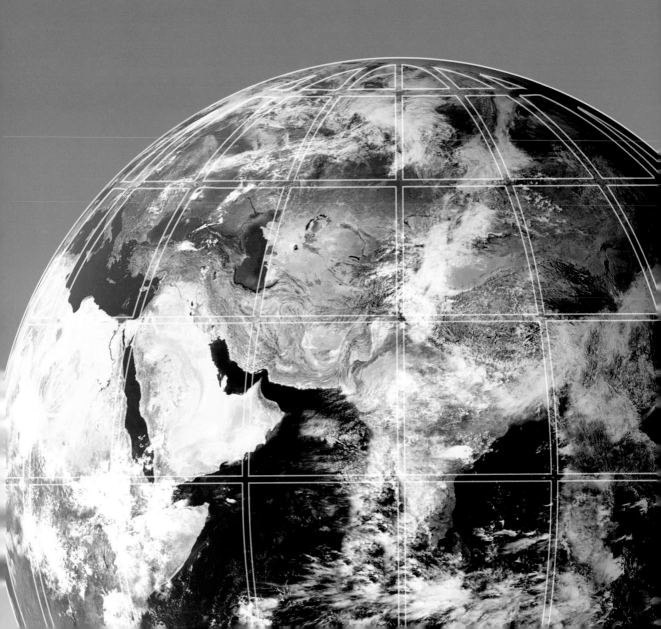

The Unique Polar Regions

In part because their temperatures are often below the freezing point of water, the polar regions are very different from any other part of the world. Their remote locations, oceanic environments, and atmospheric circulation patterns keep them somewhat isolated from the rest of the world. The Antarctic is especially isolated because it is surrounded by the world's most rapid ocean current and because it is so distant from the developed regions of the planet.

THE POLES AND THE POLAR REGIONS

The polar regions refer to the areas surrounding the north and south poles. The North Pole, also called True North, is the northernmost point where the planet's axis of rotation passes through the Earth. From the true North Pole, everywhere else is south. The South Pole is the North Pole's mirror image—the southernmost point of the Earth's surface where the planet's axis of rotation passes through.

Each of these poles has another pole located near it: the magnetic north and south poles. Seen in a diagram, the Earth's magnetic field appears as though a dipole magnet were running through the planet. At the north magnetic pole, all the magnetic field lines point downward into the Earth. At the south magnetic pole, all the magnetic field lines emerge upward from the Earth. The difference between the magnetic north pole and true North Pole is called *magnetic declination*.

The polar regions—the areas surrounding the True North and True South Poles—are defined by their **latitude**, which is the distance north or south of the Equator as measured in degrees. Earth is divided into five imaginary circles that run east-west around its mass. The central

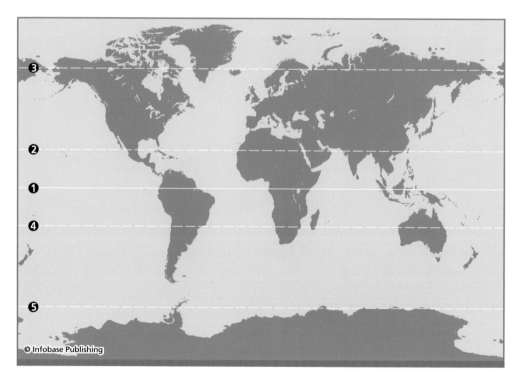

World map with the five imaginary circles: (1) the Equator, in the center (0°N); (2) the Tropic of Cancer (23° 26' 22" N) and (3) the Arctic Circle (66° 33' 38" N), in the Northern Hemisphere; and (4) the Tropic of Capricorn (23° 26' 22" S) and (5) the Antarctic Circle (66° 33' 38" S), in the Southern Hemisphere.

circle is the Equator, which is at 0°N (or, zero degree latitude north). The **Northern Hemisphere** lies between the Equator, and the North Pole and the **Southern Hemisphere** lies between the Equator and the South Pole. Each hemisphere is divided into equal thirds, and each third is bound by a circle around the globe. The two tropical circles located just north and south of the Equator are called the Tropic of Cancer and the Tropic of Capricorn. The two circles located just north and south of the poles are the Arctic Circle and the Antarctic Circle.

This discussion will focus on the territory that lies on the pole-ward sides of the Arctic and Antarctic Circles, known as the **Arctic** and the **Antarctic**, respectively. Portions of the countries of Russia, Canada, the United States (Alaska), Greenland (a territory of Denmark), Iceland, Norway, Sweden, and Finland are in the Arctic. (Notably, 20% of Russia, including much of the region called Siberia, lies north of the Arctic Circle.) Most of the Antarctic region contains the continent of Antarctica, a nearly circular landmass with a peninsula that extends northward toward South America. Antarctica is not owned by any nations and is, by international agreement, to be used only for peaceful, scientific purposes.

POLAR LIGHT AND HEAT

The essential trait of the polar regions is the tremendous variation in sunlight they receive over the course of a year. This happens for the same reason that the Earth has seasons: The angle of the planet's axis of rotation changes relative to its plane of orbit around the Sun. Earth orbits the Sun once each year and rotates on its axis once each day. The axis of rotation is tilted approximately 23.5° relative to its plane of orbit around the Sun. (This is also called the axial tilt.) At any given time, the part of the planet that points toward the Sun receives more solar radiation; this area changes as the Earth revolves during its orbit.

On June 21 or 22, a date that is called the **summer solstice**, the North Pole is tilted toward the Sun. The Sun appears at its farthest point north in the sky and is also at its highest point of the year when observed from the North Pole. (During summer solstice, the Sun's rays are vertical to the Earth at the Tropic of Cancer.) Six months later, on December 21 or 22—the **winter solstice**—the South Pole will have tilted toward the Sun. The Sun appears farthest south and is at its highest point when observed from the South Pole. (The Sun's rays are vertical at the Tropic of Capricorn.) The midway points between the solstices, when the Sun shines directly over the Equator, are autumnal or fall **equinox** (September 22 or 23) and vernal or spring equinox (March 21 or 22) in the Northern Hemisphere. In the Southern Hemisphere, the equinox dates are reversed, with vernal equinox arriving in September and autumnal equinox in March.

At the North Pole, the Sun rises on vernal equinox and does not set until autumnal equinox. During that same time, the South Pole lies in total darkness. The opposite is true in the time between autumnal and vernal equinoxes. At the poles, therefore, the Sun rises and sets only once a year, and the polar day and polar night last for six months each. During the polar day, the Sun never gets too high in the sky, but circles around the horizon, reaching its highest point on the summer solstice. During the polar night, the Sun never rises above the horizon, although the sky may show twilight some of the time. The darkest night is the winter solstice, when the Sun is at its farthest point from that pole.

Moving toward the Equator from the poles, both day and night become more like what most people are used to. The Arctic and Antarctic Circle regions have only one extended day and night each: The Sun is up continuously for one 24-hour period at the summer solstice and down for one 24-hour period at the winter solstice. At the Equator, days and nights are each nearly 12 hours long year round, and the midday Sun is always overhead. Locations along the Equator, then, receives roughly the same amount of sunlight all year long.

Because of the way the Earth's axis tilts throughout the year, the amount of solar radiation received by different parts of the Earth is very different. Each pole receives nearly all of its radiation during only half the year. Even then, because the Sun never rises very high in the polar

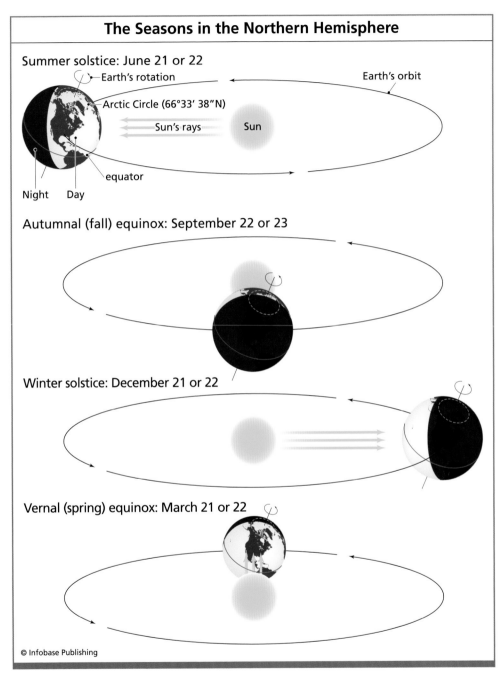

The Seasons in the Northern Hemisphere

Summer solstice: June 21 or 22

Earth's rotation

Earth's orbit

Arctic Circle (66°33′ 38″N)

Sun's rays

Sun

equator

Night   Day

Autumnal (fall) equinox: September 22 or 23

Winter solstice: December 21 or 22

Vernal (spring) equinox: March 21 or 22

© Infobase Publishing

The seasons in the Northern Hemisphere. The North Pole is always light at the summer solstice and always dark at the winter solstice.

Common Surfaces and Their Albedo

SURFACE	ALBEDO (%)	SURFACE	ALBEDO (%)
Earth, average	30	Farmland	15
Moon, average	7	Forest	3 to 10
Fresh snow	75 to 95	City, tropical region	12
Antarctica	80	Swampland	9 to 14
Clouds	30 to 90	City, northern region	7
Desert	25	Bare dirt	5 to 40
Beach	25	Ocean	3.5
Grassy field	10 to 30		

Source: C. Donald Ahrens, Meteorology Today: An Introduction to Weather, Climate, and the Environment. *6th ed. Belmont, Calif.: Brooks/Cole, 2000.*

sky, the amount of solar radiation the region receives remains relatively small. Also, whereas the Sun's rays come straight downward at the Equator, near the poles, the rays come in at an angle and so are filtered through a thicker portion of the Earth's **atmosphere** before they reach the ground. (An atmosphere is the mixture of the gases and particles that surround a planet or a moon.) For these reasons, the higher latitudes receive much less solar radiation each year than the lower latitudes.

Because the polar regions receive relatively little solar radiation, their surfaces, whether land or water, are covered with ice or snow much or all of the year. This accounts for the differences in solar energy that are reflected or absorbed by the ground surfaces on other parts of the planet. When polar ground surface reflects radiation back into the atmosphere, that radiation remains as light and does not warm the area. When a ground surface is able to absorb the radiation, the energy is converted to heat, and the area becomes warmer. The type of ground cover is extremely important because of **albedo**, which is the amount of light a surface reflects. As can be seen in the table on page 8, different types of ground surfaces have very different albedo. Ice and snow, for example, have very high albedo and reradiate most of the sunlight they receive into the atmosphere as light. Soil and vegetation absorb much of the solar energy they receive and radiate some of it back into the atmosphere as heat, so they have lower albedo. Seawater has the lowest albedo: The oceans absorb much of the solar radiation they receive and radiate only some of it back into space as heat. The

The Aurora

One of the most the spectacular features of the polar regions is the **aurora**. The aurora can be brilliant—with streamers, arcs, or fog-like bursts of light, sometimes in white and sometimes in colors—punctuating the night. These lights are called the *aurora borealis* or northern lights in the Northern Hemisphere and the *aurora australis* or southern lights in the Southern Hemisphere. The aurora is caused by the Earth's magnetic field, which channels the electrically charged particles of the incoming solar wind toward the North and South Poles. As these particles travel through the ionosphere, the part of the Earth's atmosphere where free **electrons** (tiny negatively charged particles) move as electric currents, they collide with the atmospheric gases, causing them to light up the sky. Each gas emits its own **wavelength** of light: For example, oxygen emits green or red light, and nitrogen emits red

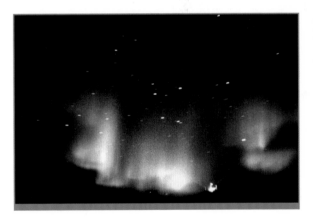

The aurora australis over South Pole Station in the 1997 Southern Hemisphere winter. The brilliant aurora forms as particles from the solar wind collide with gases in the atmosphere, causing them to emit lights of different wavelengths. *(Lieutenant Mark Boland / NOAA Corps)*

or violet. (A wavelength is the length of one wave—the distance from crest to crest or trough to trough.)

high albedo of the polar regions, therefore, contributes to the discrepancy in heat between those regions and lands at lower latitudes.

ATMOSPHERIC AND OCEANIC CIRCULATION

The imbalance of heat between the low and high latitudes due to the amount of solar radiation that comes in drives the motions of the atmosphere. Atmospheric circulation takes place in the lower atmosphere, or **troposphere**, the area located beneath the upper atmosphere, or **stratosphere**. The circulation occurs in six great **convection cells**. Each hemisphere contains three of them. An atmospheric convection cell is a circuit in which warm air rises to the top of the troposphere in one location; moves horizontally and, as it cools, sinks in another location; and then warms as it moves horizontally to its original location.

As air travels horizontally along the ground, it creates wind. The planet's major wind belts are created near the ground by the bases of the six great convection cells: The bases of the first two belts are the trade winds, between the Equator and 30°N and 30°S; the bases of the next two belts are the **westerly winds** that blow between 30° and about 50° to 60°N and 50° to 60°S; and, finally, the polar easterlies are the bottoms of the cells that blow between 60°N and the North Pole and 60°S and the South Pole. The large contrasts in the air masses that meet at 50° to 60°N and 50° to 60°S—one air mass coming from its respective pole and the other coming indirectly from the Equator—result in enormous storms that create a great

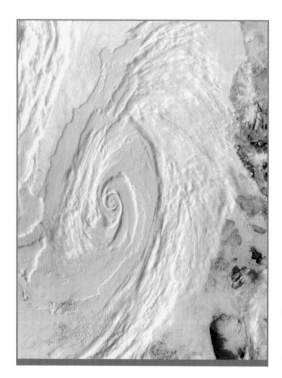

A low-pressure system over the Arctic Ocean looks like a frozen hurricane. *(Jeff Schmaltz / Aqua / MODIS / NASA)*

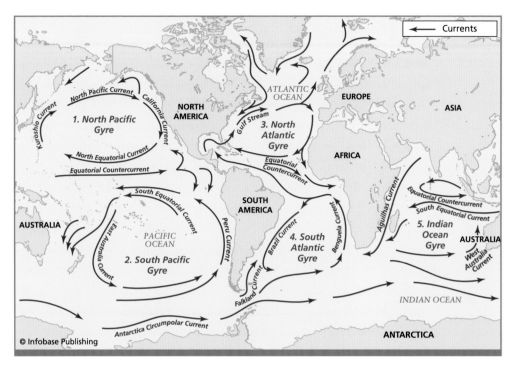

The major surface ocean currents. The five gyres are the North and South Pacific, the North and South Atlantic, and the Indian. The Antarctic Circumpolar Current moves clockwise around Antarctica and is the only surface current that is uninterrupted by land.

deal of wind and some precipitation; but very little of this precipitation reaches the continental interiors, however.

Understanding atmospheric circulation is important for understanding the polar regions for two reasons: Air circulates all around the Earth, and all air (and whatever it carries with it) eventually passes near the poles. Also, air circulation distributes heat around the Earth, which helps to keep the planet's temperature more even, though by no means entirely so.

It is the way the atmosphere moves that drives the movement of ocean currents. Winds push seawater so that the main surface ocean currents travel in the same directions as the major wind belts. The westerly winds drag North Pacific water from west to east, for example, while the trade winds move surface currents from east to west. But, unlike air, which can move freely over continents, oceanic currents must turn when they run into continents. Thus, most of the large oceanic currents become part of great loops of water known as **gyres**. Only one current travels freely around the Earth without running into a continent. Called the **Antarctic Circumpolar Current**, it flows endlessly between Antarctica and the tips of the southern continents of Australia, South America, and South Africa.

Ocean currents also flow vertically in all oceans, including the Arctic and Southern Oceans. **Upwelling** occurs where seawater flows from the ocean depths up to the surface. Upwelling water is nutrient-rich because it comes from the deep ocean, where over many decades or centuries the remains of dead plants and animals falling from the surface have collected and where there are few organisms to utilize them. (**Nutrients** are biologically important substances that are critical to living organisms.) Upwelling zones are often rich with life.

WRAP-UP

The polar regions are unique for a number of important reasons. Because each pole is tilted away from the Sun for half of the year, and because sunlight must travel through a large wedge of atmosphere, these high-latitude locations receive much less solar energy and are cold when compared to the rest of the Earth. The discrepancy in the amount of heat found in the low and high latitudes is responsible for oceanic and atmospheric circulation patterns. These atmospheric currents move heat from the low to the high latitudes, moderating, but not evening out, global temperatures. Because the polar regions are so cold, they are covered with ice and snow. These white surfaces have very high albedo and reflect rather than absorb solar radiation, further decreasing the amount of solar energy that these regions can hold. Where ice melts and dark ground or seawater is exposed, the change in albedo can have an important effect on the climate. The circulation of both the atmosphere and the ocean also plays a major role in the conditions in both polar regions by evening out temperatures to some degree.

The Nature of the Arctic and Antarctic

The Arctic consists of the land and ocean that lies north of the Arctic Circle. The Antarctic, which lies south of the Antarctic Circle, is quite a different environment from the Arctic: Among its other aspects, that region is colder and more remote. These differences will be explored further in the following chapter. Ice in many forms plays an important role in both of these regions.

THE ARCTIC OCEAN

The North Pole is found approximately at the center of the world's smallest ocean, the Arctic Ocean. At 5,440,000 square miles (14,056,000 square kilometers), this body of water is one-sixth the area of the second smallest ocean, the Indian, but is five times larger than the largest sea, the Mediterranean. The Arctic is ringed by several shallow seas along its margin and is dotted with many islands.

Sea ice covers most of the Arctic Ocean at least 10 months out of the year. When this sea ice joins together it forms **pack ice**. Much of the ocean is covered with permanent ice, which does not go away

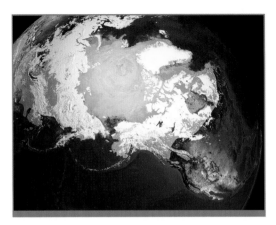

The Arctic in May 2003, as seen on a surface temperature map, MODIS Daily Snow Cover and Sea Ice Surface Temperature. The temperature differences of ice allow the image to show sea ice, ice sheets, glaciers, snow, and even buried permafrost. *(NASA / Goddard Space Flight Center Scientific Visualization Studio)*

but whose thickness increases and decreases with the seasons. Permanent ice can be up to 10 to 13 feet (3 to 4 meters) thick, with ridges up to 66 feet (20 m) thick. Some sea ice is seasonal, reaching its greatest extent in March or April and shrinking to its minimum extent in September. This seasonal ice reaches only about 3 feet (1 m) in thickness. Permanent sea ice in the Arctic Ocean extends south to about 75°N latitude, while seasonal ice reaches latitudes between 60° to 75°N. Sea ice rarely appears below 60°N, except in enclosed bays and seas. Semipermanent open regions of water can be found within the pack ice. The Arctic Ocean is icelocked at least from October to June, but some parts remain inaccessible to shipping throughout the year.

The sea ice that covers the Arctic Ocean insulates its water from the atmosphere. With its high albedo, sea ice reflects incoming solar radiation back into space, which keeps the environment from getting warm. The ice cover also prevents the ocean water from losing its heat to the atmosphere. The pack ice that covers the ocean reduces the exchange of energy between the ocean and atmosphere by about 100 times. Pack ice also restricts the **evaporation** of surface water (the change in state from a liquid to a gas). By blocking the wind from reaching the ocean surface, the ice also prevents the mixing and distribution of the ocean's nutrients and gases that are essential to living organisms. Pack ice also blocks light from the water, which prevents **photosynthesis** by plants and **algae**. (Photosynthesis is the production of sugar [food energy] and oxygen [O_2] from CO_2 and water [H_2O] in the presence of sunlight. Algae are aquatic, photosynthetic organisms but are not plants, however.)

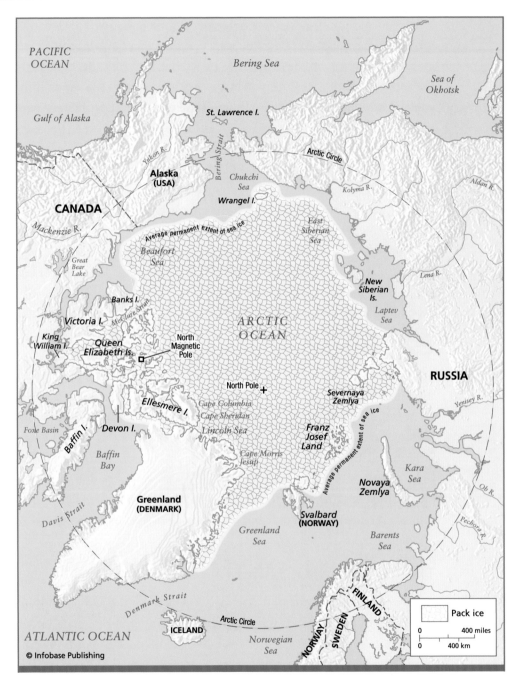

A map of the Arctic region including major landmasses, islands, the Arctic Ocean, bays and seas, the magnetic and true north poles, and the apparent extent of permanent sea ice.

Because liquid water is much warmer than ice, the Arctic Ocean is a tremendous heat source for the north polar region. Where the ocean is covered by ice, its heat actually melts the ice from the bottom. If the ice is thin, this heat may melt the ice away where the ice is thin, causing a reduction in albedo. In ice-free areas, the warm water heats the surrounding air and moderates polar air temperatures. Because oceans are important sources of moisture to the atmosphere, much of the Arctic region's precipitation falls near the Arctic Ocean. Precipitation is more likely to fall in the summer, when the weather is foggier, damper, and, surprisingly, much stormier. Winter weather over the Arctic Ocean is extremely cold and dry.

The Arctic Ocean is somewhat separated from the rest of the oceans, primarily by the continental landmasses of North America, Greenland, and Eurasia. Although Arctic Ocean waters are not freely exchanged with waters of the Pacific and Atlantic to the south, the Norwegian surface current and various deep-water currents flow in from the Atlantic. The Greenland current provides the major seawater outflow. Significantly less water flows through the Bering Strait from the Pacific Ocean.

Water also flows into the Arctic Ocean in rivers that drain from the surrounding landmasses. By far, the largest portion of the Arctic Ocean is bordered by Russia, and most of Russia's rivers and streams drain from Siberia into the Arctic Ocean. The Siberian rivers drain an area of 3 million square miles (8 million sq. km) that includes some major industrial cities, which contributes to the ocean's pollution problems.

THE GREENLAND ICE SHEET

Another large portion of the Arctic is covered by the Greenland ice sheet, one of the world's two **ice sheets**. (The other is the much larger Antarctic ice sheet.) An ice sheet is a type of enormous **glacier** (a moving body of ice that persists over time) and is defined as covering an area greater than 19,305 square miles (50,000 sq. km). Over 60% of the planet's freshwater is trapped in glaciers. Together, the Greenland and Antarctic ice sheets hold nearly 70% of this freshwater and cover about 10% of the surface. **Ice caps** are similar to ice sheets but are smaller. Both ice sheets and ice caps flow outward from an area where snow accumulation is greatest. They cover large regions of relatively flat ground, burying the underlying terrain.

The Greenland ice sheet is twice the size of California: about 1,570 miles (2,500 km) long and 600 miles (970 km) wide at its widest, for a total area of more than 650,000 square miles (1.7 million sq. km). Its average thickness is 5,800 feet (1,760 m) but reaches 11,000 feet (3,350 m) at its center. The Greenland ice sheet holds enough water to fill the Gulf of Mexico. It is confined by coastal mountains on the east and west. Like other ice sheets and ice caps, Greenland feeds smaller glaciers around its margins. The lowest annual temperature on the Greenland ice sheet reaches about −24°F (−31°C).

An **ice shelf** is a thick, floating platform of ice that flows from a glacier onto the ocean surface. When these shelves flow into the relatively warm sea, they break into small blocks of ice known as **icebergs**. Small ice caps and glaciers are found throughout the Arctic Ocean.

ARCTIC PERMAFROST

Much of the ground beneath the Arctic is perennially frozen. This feature is known as **permafrost** and is defined as soil that remains below 32°F (0°C) for at least two years. It is found beneath about one-quarter of the Northern Hemisphere's land, including that covered by glaciers. Permafrost is found beneath 85% of the ground in Alaska, and beneath 55% of both Russia and Canada.

In permafrost regions, the surface layer thaws in the summer, allowing plants to grow, but refreezes each winter. This surface layer—also known as the active layer—extends down to depths ranging from a few inches (cm) to several yards (m). The active layer responds to changes in the climate by expanding downward as surface air temperatures rise. Permanently frozen ground begins at a depth of 2 to 12 feet (0.6 to 4 m). When permafrost forms, the highest level freezes first, and then the freezing spreads downward. Usually water ice is present, but even without water, the rock or soil may freeze anyway. Engineers encounter serious challenges when building on permafrost. Sometimes a building's heating system will cause the permafrost to melt, which can undermine the structure's foundation, for example.

Permafrost is continuous nearer the pole but becomes discontinuous at lower latitudes. It can be thin or extremely thick. For example, it reaches a depth of 2,100 feet (650 m) at the high latitude of Prudhoe Bay, Alaska. Scientists estimate that it took one-half million years for this deep permafrost to form. It reaches a depth of 4,510 feet (1,493 m) in the northern Lena and Yana River basins in Siberia. Deeper permafrost has not thawed since the last ice age, over 10,000 years ago. Portions of it even extend offshore beneath the Arctic Ocean, a phenomenon that can be found nowhere else on Earth.

ANTARCTICA

Antarctica is the world's southernmost continent. It is also the smallest, after Australia and Europe. In addition to its size, Antarctica has the distinction of being the coldest, driest place on Earth.

Antarctica is covered by the Antarctic ice sheet, which, at 7 million cubic miles (30 million cubic km), contains about 90% of the world's total ice. If this ice sheet were to melt, the seas would rise by over 200 feet (60 m). This enormously thick ice sheet gives Antarctica the highest average elevation of any continent: 7,544 feet (2,300 m) above sea level. The average ice thickness is 6,500 feet (2,000 m). The thickest layer is found at Wilkes Land, at 15,669 feet (4,776 m) thick. Antarctic ice is so deep in places that scientists using advanced geophysical equipment have discovered mountain ranges and other geologic features buried beneath the ice sheet.

The 1,900 mile (3,000 km) long Transantarctic Mountains split the Antarctic continent into eastern and western sides. East Antarctica, the larger side, is dominated by a thick ice plateau that lies atop the continental mainland. West Antarctica, the smaller side, is a chain of mountainous islands and intervening water covered by ice. A portion of West Antarctica, the Antarctic Peninsula, extends far outward toward South America and is a collection of islands, mountain ranges, and

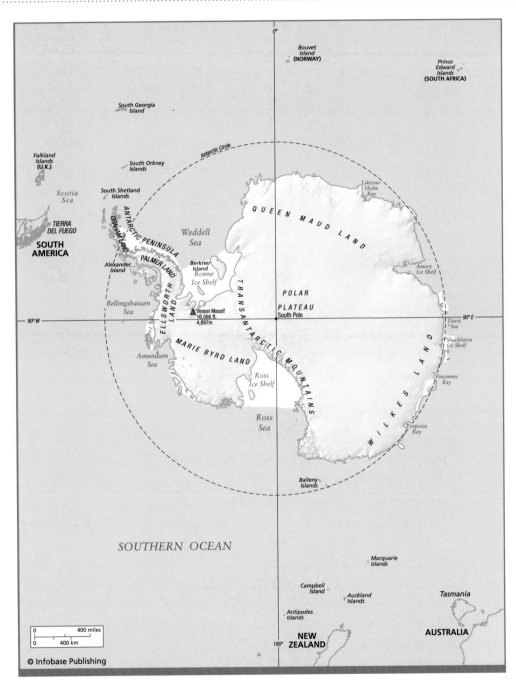

A map of the Antarctic showing the major regions of the continent, including the Antarctic Peninsula; the Southern Ocean; the seas; ice shelves; islands; and the southern tips of South America, New Zealand, and Australia.

Icebergs grounded on Pennel Bank, Ross Sea, Antarctica. *(Michael Van Woert / NOAA NESDIS, ORA)*

glaciers. The continent has two deep seas that form embayments called the Ross and the Weddell. All around the continent, glaciers flow into the sea and calve to form icebergs, which sometimes ram up against ice shelves, as seen in the photo on page 20. These ice shelves float out above the Ross and Weddell seas.

Antarctica is much colder than the Arctic, with an average annual temperature of −58°F (−50°C). The average winter temperature of the frigid continental interior ranges from −40° to −94°F (−40° to −90°C) and reaches an average of around 32°F (0°C) during the summer. Antarctica holds the record for the coldest temperature ever, recorded in 1983 at Vostok Station in East Antarctica: −129°F (−89.6°C). Antarctic temperatures are lower than Arctic temperatures because of the continent's greater elevation: The air above it is cooler, just as it would be over high mountain ranges such as the Rockies. Also, while the Arctic is warmed by the Arctic Ocean, the Antarctic is receives no warmth from its land mass. Furthermore, the sea ice that surrounds Antarctica in winter blocks much of the heat from the nearby Southern Ocean. Still, the ocean's heat does manage to warm the coastal regions somewhat, so that area is warm and wet when compared to the interior. Winter coastal temperatures range from −4° to −22°F (−20° to −30°C), with summer temperatures that reach as high as 40°F (9°C). The warmest part of Antarctica is the peninsula, which has average summer temperatures at around 35°F (2°C).

The air above Antarctica is so cold that it can hold little moisture, which is why the continent receives very little precipitation. In fact, Antarctica is the world's largest desert. Only about 2 inches (50 millimeters) of precipitation falls a year on the coldest part of the plateau, nearly all of it as snow. Near the coast, where the air is wetter, about 20 to 40 inches (50 to more than 100 cm) of precipitation falls each year. The amount of snowfall, averaged over the entire continent, totals about 6.5 inches (17 mm) per year. Permafrost lies beneath the entire continental surface.

THE SOUTHERN OCEAN

The Southern Ocean around Antarctica was recognized as the world's fifth ocean in 2000. Smaller than the Pacific, Atlantic, and Indian, but slightly larger than the Arctic, it is slightly less than 1.5 times the area of the United States. The Southern Ocean incorporates water from the southern reaches of the three largest oceans and is defined by the Antarctic Circumpolar Current.

The Antarctic Circumpolar Current has 100 times the flow volume of all the world's rivers combined. Its swift current effectively separates Antarctica from the rest of the world's surface oceans and is generated by westerly winds that travel unimpeded around the continent. With no land to slow them down, these winds, on average, are the strongest on Earth. The combination of the extreme winds and the large, swift ocean current have created intensely stormy seas in the Southern Ocean that have protected Antarctica from human development for much of its history.

The Southern Ocean is covered with so much sea ice in winter that it more than doubles the size of the Antarctic continent. Much of this sea ice, however, melts each Antarctic summer. By March, the ice pack is around 1 million square miles (2.6 million sq. km), but by September, the end of the Antarctic winter, it is about seven times larger, spreading to 7.2 million square miles (18.8 million sq. km). Sea temperatures vary from about 28° to 50°F (−2 to 10°C), with some surface areas measuring well below freezing. Icebergs detaching from the Antarctic ice sheet float throughout these seas, making travel even more dangerous.

WRAP-UP

The Arctic and Antarctic are different from the rest of the world—they are extremely cold and shrouded in ice, have day lengths up to six months long, and are relatively isolated. These two regions are also very different from each other. The Arctic is primarily an ocean surrounded by land. This ocean receives water from the Atlantic and, to a much lesser extent, from the Pacific to the south and from the rivers that run off of the surrounding landmasses. The Antarctic, on the other hand, is a continent surrounded by water. The Southern Ocean, which is defined by the Antarctic Circumpolar Current, isolates the continent from the rest of the world. The Antarctic is not only more remote, it is colder and much less hospitable than the Arctic.

Life on Land
in the Polar Regions

Earth's plants, animals, and other life forms live together in **ecosystems**—all the organisms that live in an area along with the water, land, and atmosphere they need to sustain them. Ecosystems exist on many scales: They can be as small as a flea's intestines or as large as a river, including all its tributaries and all of the land that drains into it. The entire Earth is also an ecosystem. Ecosystems, therefore, can be nested inside each other. The total number of **species** found in an ecosystem indicates its level of **biodiversity**. (A species is a classification of organisms that includes those that can or do interbreed and produce fertile offspring.)

On land, when ecosystems that have similar climate and organisms are taken together, they make up a **biome**. Polar ecosystems have very low biodiversity in comparison with more temperate ecosystems such as tropical rain forests or coral reefs. Nonetheless, many unique and interesting creatures make the polar ecosystems their home.

FOOD CHAINS AND FOOD WEBS

In every ecosystem, food energy passes from one level to another. Each level is called a **trophic level**, and organisms at one trophic level pass energy to organisms at the next trophic level. This passing of energy is described as the **food chain**.

At the base of every food chain—the first trophic level—live the **primary producers**. Most of them are photosynthetic plants and algae. Nearly all primary producers use photosynthesis to create food energy. The second trophic level consists of primary **consumers**, or **herbivores**, which are plant- or algae-eating animals. The third trophic level consists of the first-level **carnivores**, which are the animals that eat the herbivores. Animals that hunt other animals are known as **predators.** The animals they hunt are their **prey**. At the end of all food chains, usually at the third, fourth, or, more rarely, the fifth or sixth trophic levels, are the top carnivores: those animals that eat one or more of the organisms in underlying trophic levels but who are not themselves food for predators. **Scavengers** consume plant or animal tissue that is already dead.

The food chain implies that all organisms eat from only one trophic level, but many organisms, including humans, eat from multiple trophic levels. Therefore, the interactions between organisms are better described as a **food web**. Food webs can be simple, with only a few species, or they can be extremely complicated, with thousands of species involved.

Food chains are ordinarily short because most food energy is not passed along to the next trophic level but is used by an organism for its own life processes, such as reproduction. It is likely that less than 10% of the total food energy that is consumed is ever passed from one trophic level to the next. The higher an organism lives on the food chain, the more prey it needs to meet its energy requirements. In addition, the more difficult it is for an organism to capture enough prey, the smaller the population of hunters will be. Top carnivores, therefore, are fairly rare and must cover a wide area to meet their nutritional needs. Marine food chains have more trophic levels than terrestrial ones because of the abundance of organisms in the sea. Polar bears (*Ursus maritimus*), carnivorous whales, and humans (*Homo sapiens*) that are at the top of the marine food web may live at the fifth or sixth trophic level.

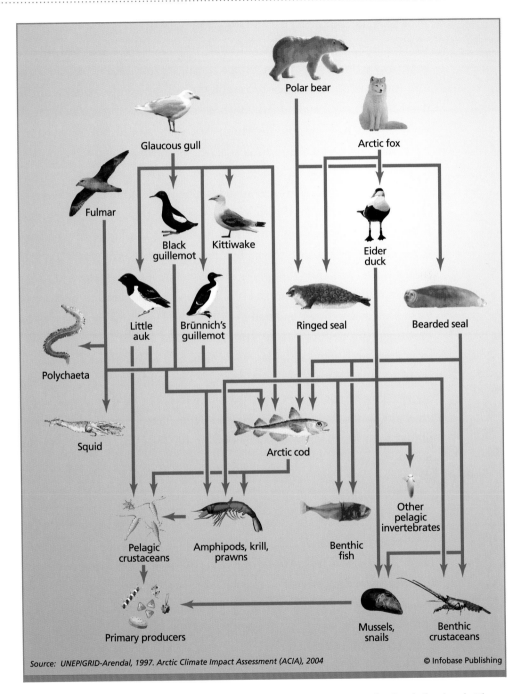

Source: UNEP/GRID-Arendal, 1997. Arctic Climate Impact Assessment (ACIA), 2004

© Infobase Publishing

Primary producers such as phytoplankton and zooplankton support the Arctic food web. These organisms are followed by small fish and invertebrates, larger fish, seabirds, seals, land mammals such as foxes, and finally polar bears and Inuit (not shown) at the highest trophic level. There are five or six trophic levels represented here, more than nearly all other food webs.

Although energy can only travel up a food chain, nutrients and water are recycled between different trophic levels. **Decomposers** such as bacteria and fungi break down organic matter (dead plant and animal tissue and waste products) into nutrients, which can be used by plants to make food. Without decomposers, each food chain would move in only one direction: Nutrients would not be recycled back into the system, and life on Earth would have ended soon after it began.

A change in one species in a food web will affect the other species in that web. For example, if a species at the third trophic level decreases in population or dies out, other species at that trophic level will have more predators chasing them, but they also will have more prey of their own to eat. How this plays out—whether the population of other species in the food web increases or decreases—depends on many factors. The food web will not collapse from the loss of one species unless that organism is a **keystone species**, named for the top center block in a stone arch that holds the other blocks in place (if the keystone is removed, the arch will fall). A top carnivore often acts as a keystone species, but keystone species also can include predators that keep prey animal populations from growing too high, large herbivores that keep plant life in balance, or organisms low in the food web that support the rest of the web.

POLAR ECOSYSTEMS

In the extremely harsh conditions of the polar regions, polar organisms have developed **adaptations** that allow them to remain active during the months of darkness and extreme cold, or they have evolved to avoid these conditions by hibernating or migrating to warmer climates. (An adaptation is a structural or behavioral modification that is passed from generation to generation.)

Due to the harsh conditions, polar ecosystems are relatively simple, with low primary productivity and low species diversity. Simple ecosystems tend to be less stable than more complex ecosystems: Each species is more important to the food web because of the relative few species that make up the food web overall. For example, when conditions are good for small mammals, the population of lemmings, an Arctic prey species, explodes. This results in a rapid increase in predator species such as snowy owls and Arctic foxes. When conditions decline

Adaptation and Evolution

Evolution is responsible for the incredible diversity of life found on Earth. Evolution means change over time, so the theory of evolution describes how creatures changed over time to become successful in the extraordinary number of **habitats** available to them. (A habitat is the place in which an organism lives, as defined by its climate, resource availability, and predators, to name just a few factors.) Habitats are as different from each other as Arctic tundra, the Kalahari desert, a tropical rain forest, and deep sea trenches. Each habitat is full of organisms that are uniquely suited for those conditions. If the environment changes, a species must adapt to the new conditions: In other words, it must evolve. As Charles Darwin, originator of the theory of evolution, said, "It is not the strongest of the species that survives, nor the most intelligent that survives. It is the one that is the most adaptable to change."

Natural selection is the mechanism for evolution laid out by Darwin. The naturalist recognized that the world is a dangerous place: Organisms must compete for food, shelter, living space, and mates.

Many young organisms will be eaten by predators or will die in a harsh environment before they reach reproductive age. Because of this, each generation produces more offspring than are needed to replace the parents. The traits of these young organisms are different: Some are faster, or have more camouflaged coloring, or have longer necks or tongues. Because of this (and a bit of chance), some offspring have an edge in competing for resources and avoiding predators. These young are *more likely* to survive to reproduce and pass on their favorable traits to their offspring. The organisms that are less fit for their environment are likely not to survive to reproduce. Over time, the favorable traits are selected for and the unfavorable traits die out.

Entirely new traits are introduced into a species' **genes**—the unit of inheritance that may be passed on to the next generation and that determines a particular trait—by **mutation**. Mutations are random, and most are neutral or harmful. Occasionally, one is beneficial and helps a species adapt to its environment. If enough changes take place over time, a new species will arise.

for small mammals, there are few lemmings and fewer predators. By contrast, a change in the population of a single species in a tropical rain forest does not have such great effects.

ARCTIC TERRESTRIAL LIFE

The **tundra** biome refers to land where the ground is frozen much of the year instead of being permanently covered by ice. It is estimated that 1,700 species of plants and 48 species of land mammals live in this biome. When compared with an estimated 5 to 50 million species of organisms in tropical rain forests, tundra biodiversity is very low.

Winters in the tundra biome are frigid: Temperatures average −18°F (−28°C) but dip as low as −94°F (−70°C). Summer temperatures average 35° to 41°F (2° to 5°C) and must rise above freezing for at least one month for tundra plant to grow. The environment is very dry: About 6 to 10 inches (50 to 250 mm) of precipitation falls each year, mostly as snow. Winds are high, reaching speeds of 30 to 60 miles per hour (48 to 97 km/h).

These severe conditions determine the types of plants that can live in the tundra biome. Tundra plants grow small and close to the ground where the air is somewhat warmer and calmer. These plants must be adapted for dark, cold winters. Most of them lie dormant during the long sunless months when they cannot photosynthesize. During the lingering summer days, plants grow rapidly, and the tundra biome flourishes. When the thin active zone thaws, the water trapped above the main permafrost layer makes the ground very wet, creating marshes, lakes, bogs, and streams. Insects time their life cycles for the spring bloom, and in summer, the air is alive with buzzing mosquitoes and other winged insects. Birds and large mammals emerge from hibernation or migrate back to the region from their warmer winter habitat. However, the growing season is typically only 50 to 60 days long, so despite the seasonal abundance, annual productivity is low.

Conditions vary from the North Pole southward through the Arctic, and the numbers and diversity of plants vary, too. The higher latitude Arctic has shorter, cooler, and drier summers, and biodiversity is lower.

Like deciduous trees, tundra brush turns colors in autumn. *(Graphicjackson / Dreamstime.com)*

This region is sparsely vegetated with grasses, dryas (small herbaceous plants), sedges, and dwarf shrubs. Mosses (small, soft plants that live in clumps) and sedge-moss meadows are common in poorly drained regions. Conditions in the high latitude Arctic mountain highlands are so extreme that the vegetation is mostly found growing in cracks in the frost. Some flowers, such as the Arctic poppy (*Papaver nudicaule*), are solartropic: They track the Sun's movements across the sky so they can absorb the maximum amount of heat and light.

Conditions in the low Arctic are less severe, and most land surfaces are vegetated. The lower latitudes of the Arctic support about twice as many species of **vascular plants** as the high Arctic. (Vascular plants have roots, stems, and leaves for transporting water and food, and a cuticle that helps them resist desiccation.) The tundra has tall shrubs, such as willow (*Salix* sp.), birch (*Betula* sp.), and alder (*Alnus* sp.), and many low plants such as blueberry and cranberry (*Vaccinium* sp.) and Arctic heather (*Cassiope* sp.). Dryas and saxifraga are found in the low Arctic mountain highlands, where lichens (a fungus coupled with an algae) and mosses are also common.

No amphibians or reptiles are found in the Arctic or Antarctic due to the harsh conditions. The diversity of Arctic mammals and birds increases from north to south as the climate warms and the hours of daylight increase. The highest Arctic latitudes, above 80°N, have only a few mammal species. These animals are adapted to the most extreme conditions and include herbivores such as the musk ox (*Ovibos moschatus*), Peary caribou (*Rangifer tarandus*, subspecies *pearyi*), Arctic hare (*Lepus arcticus*), and collard lemming (*Dicrostonyx* sp.). Their predators include the wolf (*Canis lupus*), Arctic fox (*Alopex lagopus*), wolverine (*Gulo gulo*), and ermine (*Mustela erminea*). Conditions are so extreme here that when the weather becomes too harsh for too long, a population of animals such as musk ox may become locally extinct (meaning that no member of the species survives to reproduce) and will replenish only after conditions have improved to a state where others of their species can migrate in from elsewhere.

Further south, mammals can be found that also live only in the polar environment, including herbivores such as caribou (reindeer) and lemmings. There are also mammals that are common in more temperate environments, such as ground squirrels (*Spermophilus* sp.), red foxes (*Vulpes* sp.), and brown bears (*Ursus arctos*). Mammals that live primarily in warmer climates but also frequent the lower latitudes of the Arctic include moose (*Alces alces*) and snowshoe hare (*Lepus americanus*). Mountain sheep (*Ovis* sp.) and marmots (*Marmota* sp.) live in the Arctic highlands. The high summer productivity of tundra plants attracts large annual migrations of animals such as caribou (reindeer) and geese. Most caribou migrate in large herds between their summer birthing ground and their winter feeding grounds. During their migrations, the herds run through snow and tundra and swim across lakes and wide rivers. Alaska and northern Canada each support populations of about one million caribou.

Only a few species of land birds live year round in the Arctic: the ptarmigan (*Lagopus* sp.), snowy owl (*Bubo scandiacus*), gyrfalcon (*Falco rusticolus*), and raven (*Corvus corax*). Many more species migrate into the region to breed and raise young in the summer, including the Arctic redpoll (*Cardeulis hornemanni*) and snow bunting (*Plectrophenax nivalis*), and raptors such as the golden eagle (*Aquila chrysaetos*), white-tailed eagle (*Haliaeetus albicilla*), peregrine falcon (*Falco peregrinus*), and short-eared owl (*Asio flammeus*). Migrating shorebirds and waterfowl fly up the edges of continents to make their homes on the relatively warm coastlines or in lakes and wet meadows. Passerine species, such as finches and sparrows, live in the southern Arctic.

Toward the lower latitudes, the tundra biome gives way to the **boreal forest** biome, where the ground is not frozen and trees can grow. Boreal forests are dominated by fir trees, which can survive frosts. Due to the harsh conditions, boreal forests have lower species diversity than other forests.

ANTARCTIC TERRESTRIAL LIFE

Most of Antarctica is ice covered, but where it is not, conditions are more severe than in the Arctic. Life is most abundant on the Antarctic Peninsula, but even there, biodiversity is very low. Some organisms live on the ice, and portions of several islands support Antarctic tundra.

The plants are small and hardy: lichens, mosses, liverworts, and many species of algae. Antarctica has only two species of flowering plants: the Antarctic hair grass (*Deschampsia antarctica*) and Antarctic pearlwort (*Colobanthus quitensis*).

A few species of **invertebrates** (animals without backbones), single-celled protozoa, rotifers, tardigrades, nematodes, and collembolan (primitive wingless insects) live in the region. Relative to the Arctic, there are few species of insects, and most of them, such as lice, live on larger animals. Unique cyanobacteria live in rocks in the dry valleys of southern Victoria Land. They are usually dormant but come to life when melting snow provides enough moisture for them to engage in life processes.

Marine mammals and birds, including penguins, live in coastal areas and hunt from the pack ice, where they are part of the marine food web. Antarctica has no native land mammals, apparently because none could migrate the long distances from the southern continents across the stormy seas. Introduced reindeer have established colonies in a few locations. Some small mammals, such as rabbits and domestic cats, have been introduced to the small islands. (Mammals and birds are among the **vertebrates**, which also include other animals with backbones such as reptiles and amphibians.)

PEOPLE OF THE ARCTIC

Antarctica never had an **indigenous** population—meaning people who were native to the area. The region was too hostile and too inaccessible. Antarctica still does not have permanent residents and is now only a temporary home to about 4,000 scientists and scientific support staff. In contrast, about 4 million people live north of the Arctic Circle, spread over so much land that the population density is less than one person per square mile (2.5 sq. km). Nearly all of them live in settlements that range in size from large, industrialized cities to small nomadic communities.

The Arctic has been home to humans for at least 5,000 years. About 10% of the area's current inhabitants are indigenous. The Arctic has at least 30 different indigenous groups of people speaking dozens of languages. The proportion of an area's population that is made up of indigenous people varies by location: They account for 80% of the population in Greenland, 15% in Arctic Norway, and only 3% to 4% in Arctic Russia. Some of them now live an entirely modern lifestyle, while others follow at least some of their traditional ways.

Although the term *Eskimo* is still used by some to refer to Arctic people, most indigenous Arctic residents prefer to be called by the name of the group to which they belong. Traditionally, the Arctic people lived north of the tree line while other people, such as the Native Americans in North America, resided in the forests further south. Contact between the two groups of people often resulted in conflict. Arctic people utilized resources in a similar fashion to Native Americans: They hunted marine mammals, such as whales, seals, and walrus (*Odobenus rosmarus*), and land animals such as caribou and fished in streams and lakes. Their diets were heavy in fatty meats, which helped them survive the extreme cold, but light on vegetables, which grow sparsely in the Arctic region. Some people, such as the Saami, or Laplanders, herded reindeer in what is now Norway.

The largest group of indigenous Arctic people is the **Inuit**, whose population of about 155,000 is now widely distributed over northern Alaska, Canada, and Greenland. Traditionally, the Inuit were people of the snow and the sea ice on which they hunted, fished, and traveled. They hunted whales, walrus, caribou, and seals, but they would also pursue birds, small mammals, polar bears, and musk oxen, if necessary. To capture marine mammals, a hunter would head out on the water in a single-passenger sealskin boat similar to a modern kayak (In fact, kayaks were modeled after these very vessels). These boats were especially useful because they could easily be righted if they tipped over. The boat's outer hull was made of sealskin, which helped it move easily and silently through the water. Large open boats were used for transportation. Inuit hunters often pursued prey in the same manner as a polar bear, by waiting at a seal's breathing hole and spearing the animal when it emerged for air. On land, the Inuit bred huskies for use as sled dogs for traveling or for hunting. By necessity, the Inuit were very economical with their materials. They used animal tusks, hide, and bone to manufacture tents, clothes, and boats, while consuming all of the animal's edible parts. For protection, and to share resources, extended families lived together.

Inuit subsistence hunting skills continue to be passed down from generation to generation. Even today, hunting remains the basis of Inuit life. Their social structure depends on hunting and sharing food among families. While some Inuit currently engage in traditional practices, they often pursue them by using modern technologies such as snowmobiles, motorboats, and rifles.

The first known contact between the Inuit and Europeans occurred with the Vikings in Greenland. Inuit arrived in the area in about 1150, during the relatively warm Medieval Warm Period (MWP), which lasted from about 900 to 1300. There is little known about how these two groups got along: Some interactions seem to have been friendly, while others led to hostilities. The MWP was hard on the Inuit, as it made following their traditions of hunting from sea ice more difficult. The time of the Little Ice Age (LIA), lasting about 500 years beginning in the fourteenth century, was much kinder to them because of an increase in the sea ice they needed for hunting. However, the Inuit also suffered during this same period because an important source of their protein, bowhead whales (*Balaena mysticetus*), moved farther south in response to the colder weather.

Later contact with more varied groups of Europeans had mixed success. The Inuit enjoyed trading for (or perhaps stealing) metal knives and other products brought by the visitors. But, as commonly happened during contact between indigenous cultures and Europeans, the indigenous people were struck by diseases they had not previously been exposed to, and huge numbers of them died as a result. For the most part, though, people in the far north were largely left alone because there were no known riches there for the Europeans to exploit. Even into the early twentieth century, some Inuit had never come in contact with Europeans. Eventually, though, most Inuit abandoned living a fully traditional life. Modern medical care improved birth rates and lowered death rates, which allowed the population to grow too high: This meant that subsistence living could no longer feed everyone. Most Inuit gave up their nomadic way of life and moved into towns. The education they received from the dominant cultures, both secular and religious, suggested to them (often unkindly) that they become part of modern culture. In time, these extremely self-sufficient people, who were extraordinarily well adapted to their environment, became dependent on the new dominant culture.

In the 1960s, many Inuit became politically active and worked to get land settlements from the countries in which they lived. Now, the Inuit work in industries such as oil and gas and supplement their incomes by subsistence hunting. Inuit also work in the tourism industry and produce handicrafts for sale. Modern life has its benefits, but the Inuit diet of hunted game has largely been replaced by sugary and fatty packaged foods, so their health has consequently deteriorated. Unable to support themselves, many rely on welfare.

WRAP-UP

Life on land in Earth's polar regions is harsh, so the biodiversity of these areas is low in comparison to the planet's more hospitable areas. The seasonal cycles of life are very pronounced in these areas. Plants lie dormant during the winter and then grow rapidly during the very short summer season. Animals emerge from hibernation or migrate back into the area from warmer climates. Some reproduce rapidly to take advantage of the brief period of abundance. Many animals live on land but get their food mostly from the sea and so play their part in the polar marine ecosystems, which will be described in the next chapter. The indigenous people of the far north were once well tuned to this seasonal lifestyle. They ate mostly from the sea, hunting seals and whales from shore or small boats. Their lives have changed radically since their first contact with Europeans several centuries ago.

Life in the Polar Seas

While polar terrestrial life-forms may be low in number and diversity, this is not the case with polar marine organisms. This chapter explores how the oceans of the Arctic and Antarctic both have rich and varied food webs that are founded on the abundant tiny organisms that live in the lower two trophic levels. Many animals depend on these organisms for survival, and some important creatures, such as whales, migrate into these areas for summer feeding and migrate out to other destinations for winter breeding.

THE BASE OF THE POLAR MARINE FOOD WEB

Primary producers depend on sunlight and nutrients to reproduce and grow. Nutrients in the polar oceans are most abundant in upwelling zones. In the Arctic Ocean, ocean circulation is restricted by the surrounding land, so there is less nutrient upwelling than there is around Antarctica, where nutrient-rich waters are stirred by the Antarctic Circumpolar Current.

Like life on the polar landscape, life in the polar oceans is very seasonal: It flourishes whenever there is enough sunlight. A **plankton bloom** begins when the Sun climbs high enough in the sky to provide enough light for photosynthesis. **Phytoplankton** are minute marine organisms, mostly algae that produce food by photosynthesis. Phytoplankton form the lowest trophic level, which is the base of most oceanic food webs. In the Arctic Ocean, the spring phytoplankton population explosion, seen in the photo on this page, quickly uses up nutrients, resulting in a rapid population decline. In the Southern Ocean, nutrients are so abundant that they rarely become depleted, so the phytoplankton bloom lasts as long as there is enough light. As a result, productivity in the southern

A phytoplankton bloom in the Barents Sea changes the color of the sea from normal deep blue to bright blue-green due to the sunlight reflecting off the chalky shells. Franz Josef Land is in the top left corner but is obscured by clouds; Novaya Zemlya is in the top right corner. *(Jacques Descloitres, MODIS Land Rapid Response Team, NASA/GSFC)*

latitudes is higher than in the northern; but in both oceans, productivity drops to near zero once darkness sets in.

Phytoplankton provide food for tiny floating animals called **zooplankton**, the other type of **plankton**. Zooplankton populations rise shortly after the phytoplankton bloom begins to take advantage of the abundant food. Zooplankton consist of representatives of nearly every major animal group, including the larvae of much larger animals. Many zooplankton are **crustaceans**, a group that includes crabs, lobsters, and shrimp. About 70% of individual zooplankton are tiny shrimp-like copepods. The group of zooplankton called **krill** is made up of multiple species of small crustaceans that average about 2.3 inches (6 cm) long. Phytoplankton and zooplankton form the base of the Arctic and Antarctic food webs.

ARCTIC MARINE LIFE

Near shore, where the water is shallow enough for plants to be rooted and still engage in photosynthesis, marine plants thrive. Nutrients enter the Arctic Ocean from the landmasses that surround it. Many of them settle on the seafloor along the continental shelves. As a result, a great abundance and diversity of organisms exists on or in seafloor sediments. About 90% of the 5,000 species of marine invertebrates that live in the Arctic reside in or on the seafloor, but only 350 to 400 of those are found in the deep ocean basin. Larger animals that live on top of the sediment include brittle stars, sea urchins, and sea cucumbers. Animals on the continental shelf include crustaceans such as amphipods and sand fleas, polychaetes such as bristle worms, and bivalve mollusks. The bottom-dwelling organisms, in turn, support an abundance of bottom-feeding mammals such as gray whales (*Eschrichtius robustus*) and walrus. Some Arctic **benthic** organisms, which live on the bottom of the sea, are **endemic species**. Endemic species are species that are found in no other location.

Fish swim throughout the Arctic Ocean, feeding along the bottom, in the midwaters, or at the surface. However, the Arctic has no endemic fish species. Nonnative species of organisms often enter the area by way of the water that flows in from farther south. Many of these species die in the harsh conditions, but some manage to establish colonies.

Marine birds and mammals are endotherms, or warm-blooded, and have feathers or fur for insulation. Many Arctic birds, such as puffins (*Fratercula* sp.), auklets, gulls, and terns, are part of the marine food web and rely on fish and other sea creatures for their food. These birds

Arctic Seals

There are six species of seals that live at least part of their lives on Arctic ice. Their isolation makes population estimates difficult, but some are included below.

Bearded seal (*Erignathus barbatus*), lying on Bering Sea ice and showing its blubber, one of the adaptations that allow the seals to live in frigid temperatures. (*F2 / Dreamstime.com*)

- Ringed seals (*Pusa hispida*): The estimated population of these abundant seals stands at 2,000,000 worldwide. Ringed seals live close to the ice year round and spend their winters swimming beneath the ice. The animals use their claws to maintain their own breathing holes. While the ice affords the seals some protection, polar bears are often seen waiting by a breathing hole to catch a seal when it comes up to breathe. Ringed seals eat fish and other marine organisms.
- Bearded seals (*Erignathus barbatus*): Bearded seals ram their heads through the ice to maintain their breathing holes. These seals prefer broken pack ice but may live on shore or on thick ice. They migrate seasonally, heading north as the days grow longer and south as they grow shorter. Bearded seals are often seen lying on the ice and looking down into the water, ready to escape from predators at a moment's notice. These seals are a primary food source for polar bears and the Inuit people. Their population is estimated at 500,000. They are primarily bottom feeders that eat shrimp, crabs, clams, and welks, but they will also eat fish such as cod and sculpin.
- Harp seals (*Phoca groenlandica*): Currently estimated at about 5.2 million, the population of these seals has fluctuated widely with the rise and fall of commercial hunting.

(continues)

(continues)

- Hooded seals (*Cystophora cristata*): This highly migratory species of seal travels long distances to feed and dives deep for fish. The total world population is estimated at about 650,000.
- Spotted seals (*Phoca largha*): The population estimate for spotted seals is under 300,000. These seals migrate with the ice front from their wintering grounds in the Bering Sea up into the Arctic Ocean in the summer and back again. Spotted seals eat marine creatures such as fish and cephalopods. Spotted seals are not subject to the same level of predation as other seals, although humans, polar bears, sharks, Steller sea lions, brown bears, and walrus will feed on them.
- Ribbon seals (*Phoca fasciata*): These young seals were once hunted for their fur, but since the 1969 ban, the population of ribbon seals has recovered. Their predators include killer whales, sharks, and polar bears, but they spend their lives floating on pack ice away from land and therefore are not easy to hunt. Ribbon seals eat mostly fish. They live so far from people that their population is unknown but is estimated at about 250,000.

are primarily found living on sea cliffs in regions where upwelling currents provide a rich food web. Birds and some mammals can also live and nest above 75°N where upwelling currents within the small open areas in the pack ice supply a rich food source.

The Arctic is full of marine mammals, including many **pinnipeds** (seals, sea lions, walrus), and **cetaceans** (whales, dolphins, and porpoises). Most of the world's seals live close to the Arctic or Antarctic circles, where they breed on the ice. Seals and sea lions have torpedo-shaped bodies and are graceful swimmers but move awkwardly on land. Some seals endure long migrations from high latitudes, where they feed, to low latitudes, where they breed. Sea lions are streamlined, so they can dive deep for food without surfacing for many minutes at a time. Arctic ice seals are prey for humans, foxes, wolves, dogs, wolverines, large birds, and polar bears (which eat their blubber but not their meat).

Walrus are found only in the Arctic and can weigh up to two tons (1.8 metric tons). Both males and females have tusks that they use for many purposes such as pulling themselves out of the water. A walrus can rotate its hind flippers to haul itself out of the water and walk on hard surfaces; it can even use them like sled runners to glide over the sea bottom. Walrus locate clams with their heavy, muscular whisker pads. With their mouths, they dig the clams up, crush the shells, remove the meat, and spit out the inedible fragments.

Cetaceans rely heavily on the large quantities of food found in both polar oceans. Some species live in Arctic waters, while others only visit to take part in the summer bounty. A few whale species migrate thousands of miles annually, from polar ocean to polar ocean to feed, and to warmer waters to breed.

There are two main types of whales: toothed and baleen. **Toothed whales** feed mostly on fish and squid, although some eat seals. These animals use sound waves to create a picture of their environment and to stun, debilitate, or even kill their prey. The world's largest whales are the 11 species of **baleen whales**. These enormous animals use baleen, a coarse, stiff, fibrous substance, to filter krill and other zooplankton from seawater.

Another top predator of the Arctic Ocean ecosystem is the polar bear. The favorite foods of polar bears are ringed seals, bearded seals, and harp seals, which they capture as the animals poke their heads through holes in the ice to breathe. The bears prefer to eat the seals' high-calorie blubber. Like other bears, polar bears are opportunistic and will eat anything they can kill: birds, rodents, shellfish, crabs, beluga whales, walrus, and (rarely) musk oxen or even other polar bears. Polar bears will even eat trash if the opportunity presents itself. Polar bear mothers give birth to cubs every three years and nurse their young for two years.

Arctic Whales

The following species of whales live at least part of their lives in Arctic waters.

- Bowhead whales (*Balaena mysticetus*) are also called Greenland whales or Arctic whales. These are the only baleen whales that live their entire lives in Arctic waters, wintering in the southwestern Bering Sea and following the ice pack northward in the summer to hunt krill and other zooplankton. These whales can reach 66 feet (20 m) long and can dive for as long as 40 minutes. They use their massive heads to break through the ice to create breathing holes. Their blubber is thicker than that of any other animal—17 to 20 inches (43 to 50 cm).

- Beluga whales (*Delphinapterus leucas*) are smaller than most other toothed whales at 16 feet (5 m) long. The distinctive white-toothed whale lives in Arctic and sub-Arctic waters from 50° to 80°N, with one small population in the St. Lawrence River estuary and another at Saguenay fjord in Quebec. Belugas live at the edge of the ice pack, preferably in shallow coasts and river inlets. Belugas eat fish, squid, octopus, and crustaceans and spend time foraging for invertebrates at the seabed.

- Narwhals (*Monodon monoceros*) are toothed whales primarily living north of 70°N. They are 13 to 16 feet long (4 to 5 m), but males sport a distinctive 10-foot (3-m) long tusk. Narwhals feed mainly on cod that live beneath the ice but will also eat squid, shrimp, and other fish.

- Sperm whales (*Physeter macrocephalus*), the largest of the toothed whales, may reach a length of 60 feet (18 m). They live throughout the oceans. To hunt their prey of giant squid, octopus, and rays, they dive to depths of more than 3,740 feet (1,140m), the deepest of diving whales. Sperm whales have long life spans, mature slowly, give birth to few young, and nurse their young for two to three years.

Arctic marine life is also found in places where it is not expected. Tiny organisms, less than 0.04 inches (1 mm) in diameter, have been discovered in the liquid pores and channels found within sea ice. Most of them are bacteria and single-celled plants and animals. One multicellular animal, the gammaridean amphipod (*Gammarus wilkitzkii*), lives densely packed beneath the sea ice. This animal is an important food source for Arctic cod (*Boreogadus saida*), which, in turn, are the food for many other animals such as birds, seals, and whales. Thriving communities of these creatures have been found along with large numbers of jellies, squid, cod, and other animals that also find shelter beneath the pack ice.

ANTARCTIC-SOUTHERN OCEAN MARINE LIFE

Antarctic krill (*Euphausia superba*) are the keystone of the Antarctic ecosystem. These zooplankton have the greatest **biomass** (total living mass) of any single species on Earth: Collectively, they weigh about 454 million tons (500 million metric tons) and reach densities of 38 to 114 individual animals per gallon (3.8 liters). Besides feeding on phytoplankton, krill feed on the ice algae that hang beneath the pack ice.

Because of the abundance of krill, the Southern Ocean is one of the world's most productive ecosystems. Many Antarctic organisms, including squid, fishes, seabirds, penguins, seals, and some whales, feed directly on krill. The distribution of krill is affected by the distribution of sea and ice, which affects the distribution and abundance of other marine life. Some Antarctic food webs are very simple: Krill are the main food source for Adélie penguins, which are the favorite prey of leopard seals. Killer whales, in turn, eat both penguins and seals.

Numerous organisms dive deep for food in the Southern Ocean, including king penguins, seals, and whales. The large numbers, wide distribution, and high energy needs of these predators suggests that many prey organisms, such as squid and fish, live in the midwaters.

Antarctic Fish

Two hundred kinds of fish live in Antarctic waters, including many species of specialized endemic fish. As plate tectonic processes moved

Antarctic and Subantarctic Penguins

There are six species of penguins that live in the Antarctic and subantarctic. Penguins are difficult to count, and population estimates vary widely. The numbers given below are only estimates.

- Emperor penguins (*Aptenodytes forsteri*) are the largest of the species, ranging from 3 feet, 11 inches (1.27 m) to 5 feet, 4 inches (1.6 m) long and weighing up to 75 pounds (34 kilograms). Emperors eat mainly fish and squid but sometimes eat krill. These penguins were immortalized in the 2005 documentary film *March of the Penguins*, which chronicled the amazing journeys the birds must take to survive and produce healthy young. There are an estimated 220,000 breeding pairs of Emperor penguins.
- Adélie penguins (*Pygoscelis adeliae*) are highly dependent on krill for food, although they will eat fish and amphipods. There are about 4 million breeding pairs living on the Antarctic coast and nearby islands. Adélies are smaller than Emperors, averaging 28 inches (70 cm) and weighing 6.6 to 14 pounds (3 to 6.5 kg). Like Emperors, Adélies travel long distances between their rookeries and feeding grounds.
- King penguins (*Aptenodytes patagonicus*) are the second largest penguins at 3 feet (90 cm) tall and 24 to 35 pounds (11 to 16 kg). These birds eat small fish and squid and rely less on krill than many other species. Like Emperors, they walk or toboggan. The 2 million pairs of King Penguins live in the subantarctic in an environment far less harsh than the Emperors, and their ranges do not overlap.
- Macaroni penguins (*Eudyptes chrysolophus*) mostly live in the subantarctic and rely on krill, fish, and squid. These are the most numerous penguins, with over 9 million breeding pairs.

the Antarctic continent toward the South Pole, it eventually became completely surrounded by ocean water by about 33 million years ago. At that point, the fish that lived around the continent became isolated

A colony of Adélie penguins on Humble Island, in the Palmer Archipelago. *(© Gary Braasch, from the book* Earth Under Fire: How Global Warming Is Changing the World, *University of California Press, 2007)*

⊕ Chinstrap penguins (*Pygoscelis antarctica*), with 7 million breeding pairs, feed primarily on krill. The birds live in the subantarctic, midway between the Adélie penguins to the south and the Gentoo penguins to the north.

⊕ Gentoo penguins (*Pygoscelis papua*) are shy birds with the widest distribution of any penguin, living on subantarctic islands and on the Antarctic Peninsula. The roughly 300,000 breeding pairs primarily eat fish and squid.

from lower latitude relatives by the Antarctic Circumpolar Current. As temperatures decreased, these now-isolated fish either adapted to the harshening conditions or went **extinct**. The species that survived evolved unique strategies for dealing with the environment. One example of Antarctic fish that flourished are the **icefish**, a group of 200 species that are the dominant fish in that environment. Icefish feed primarily on krill, copepods, and other fish.

Antarctic fish are well adapted to cold temperatures that would freeze any low latitude fish's blood solid. Their blood fluid, or plasma, includes proteins that act like "antifreeze," lowering the temperature at which ice crystals grow. Low temperatures also make blood very viscous, which makes it very difficult to pump. Antarctic fish have adapted two strategies for dealing with this particular problem:

- Antarctic red-blooded fish have a smaller number of red blood cells per volume of circulating blood than red-blooded fish of the temperate zones, which reduces the blood's viscosity.
- Icefish blood is extremely dilute, containing only one percent cells. Icefish blood has no **hemoglobin**, the reddish molecule that distributes oxygen from an animal's lungs through its body via the blood and then carries waste gases back to the lungs. Icefish blood also has little or no **myoglobin**, the molecule that tightly binds oxygen into muscles for use during exertion. Simply put, what pumps through an icefish's body is ice water. Without the ability to distribute oxygen through their blood, icefish have other adaptations. Because gases dissolve more easily in cold water, the water that icefish swim in has high concentrations of oxygen, and the fish are able to take advantage of this. Icefish have other adaptations for gathering oxygen such as large gills, skin that contains large capillaries to increase oxygen absorption (instead of scales), larger hearts, and larger blood volumes.

The basic cell structures of Antarctic fish are also adapted to the cold. For example, microtubules, which play an important role in cell

Antarctic Seals

The five species of seals and one species of sea lion that live on Antarctic ice are listed below.

- ⊕ Southern elephant seals (*Mirounga leonine*) are the largest seals: The males reach 8 feet (5.5 m) in length with a weight of 5,000 pounds 2,270 kg). They come ashore to breed in summer but winter at sea. The population of southern elephant seals is estimated at around 600,000. These animals dive for cephalopods, large fish, and sharks.

- ⊕ Antarctic fur seals (*Arctocephalus gazella*) are also known as Kerguelen fur seals. These seals primarily eat krill, fish, and squid, about 1 ton (0.9 metric tons) per year per adult. The seals breed on ice-free islands, with 95% of them located on South Georgia, where they are thought to maintain the densest population of any marine mammals anywhere. Killer whales and leopard seals prey on young members of this species.

- ⊕ Crabeater seals (*Lobodon carcinophagus*), despite their name, filter krill from the water. These abundant animals, which total about 15 million, appear to be the second most abundant large mammal (after humans). Killer whales (orcas) prey on crabeater seals and may bump an ice floe to knock one into the water to capture it.

- ⊕ Leopard seals (*Hydrurga leptonyx*) have a population estimated at 220,000 to 440,000. Their varied diet runs to krill, fish, penguins, and other seals. They are sometimes eaten by killer whales.

- ⊕ Ross seals (*Ommatophoca rossii*) are uncommon, almost never leaving the Antarctic region. These seals dive for cephalopods and fish, with squid making up two-thirds of their diet. Ross seals are eaten by killer whales and leopard seals.

- ⊕ Weddell seals (*Leptonychotes weddellii*) are often found beneath pack ice, surfacing to breathe at cracks or holes in the ice. This frigid underwater environment is relatively free of predators. The Weddell seal population is around 800,000. Stealthy hunters, Weddell seals can flush fish out of crevices in the ice by blowing bubbles.

Southern Ocean Whales

The following species of whales live at least part of their lives in the Southern Ocean:

- Blue whales (*Balaenoptera musculus*), at 100 feet (30 m) long and 165 tons (150 metric tons) in weight, are the largest animals that ever lived, even larger than the largest dinosaurs. To survive, these baleen whales must eat 6,600 pounds (3 metric tons) of krill each day.

- Fin whales (*Balaenoptera physalus*) can grow to 88 feet (27 m) and are the second largest whales. (The weight is unknown, as a full-size adult has never been weighed.) Fin whales are found in all the world's oceans but do not live near the pack ice. Like blue whales, fin whales are migratory baleen whales.

- Humpback whales (*Megaptera novaeangliae*) feed only in summer, using their baleen to feed off the Southern Ocean zooplankton. In winter, they move to warmer waters and calve while living off their fat deposits. These enormous animals range between 40 to 50 feet (12 to 16 m) long and weigh approximately 40 tons (36 metric tons). Young humpbacks are eaten by orcas, which are predatory toothed whales.

- The two species of minke whales are the Northern (*Balaenoptera acutorostrata*) and the Southern or Antarctic (*Balaenoptera bonaerensis*). These baleen whales are relatively small—around 23 or 24 feet (6.9 to 7.4 m) and 15 tons (14 metric tons).

- Southern right whales (*Eubalaena australis*) are also large baleen whales, at 60 feet (18 m), that stay close to peninsulas and bays. They summer in the Southern Ocean and breed in winter off the southern continents.

- Sei whales (*Balaenoptera borealis*) can grow to 66 feet (20 m) and inhabit all the oceans. Sei whales feed on small fish, squid, and plankton.

- The orca or killer whale (*Orcinus orca*) is actually a large species of dolphin. Orcas live throughout all oceans and seas except near ice packs, usually in coastal areas. They eat fish, sea turtles, seabirds, pinnipeds, and manatees, and are the only species besides humans to attack large whales, which they do as a group.

division and movement, are unstable at such cold temperatures and so are different in Antarctic fish.

Penguins

Penguins are an important part of the Southern Ocean marine food web. These flightless birds are found only in the Southern Hemisphere, although the equatorial Galapagos penguin (*Spheniscus mendiculus*) may cross the Equator to feed. Many penguins feed primarily on krill, but some are important carnivores, eating fish, squid, and other, larger marine animals.

Penguins spend about half their time on land and half fishing in the ocean. The torpedo-shaped birds are dark on top and light on their bellies for camouflage. From above, their dark backs blend in with the water below; from below, their light bellies blend in with the sky above. Penguin wings are no longer adapted for flight but have evolved to become flippers that propel the birds' streamlined bodies rapidly through the seas. Many penguins dive for food. The largest penguins can dive the deepest: Emperor penguins, for example, can dive to a depth of 1,870 feet (565 m) for up to 20 minutes. On land, penguins move awkwardly, but they may walk or slide across the ice on their bellies, a mode of transportation called tobogganing. Their wings and tails help the birds to balance on land. Penguins wear a covering of outer feathers that traps a layer of air that provides buoyancy and insulation.

Only two penguin species—the Emperor and the Adélie—live on the Antarctic mainland, but others live on the Antarctic Peninsula and on subantarctic islands. The species that live farthest south are typically larger because large bodies retain heat better.

Seals

The majority of the world's seals live in the Antarctic. For millennia, these animals had a relatively easy time: There were no humans to hunt them, they were protected from other predators by sea ice, and krill were abundant. Because Antarctic seals have not been hunted as much, they are not as wary of people as other species.

Whales

Whales are particularly abundant in the Southern Ocean due to the enormous amount of krill that are available in the summer. Many large baleen whales feed in the Southern Ocean in the summer, and then migrate northward into warmer waters to calve in the winter. These baleen whales primarily eat zooplankton but may filter fish and small squid for food as well.

WRAP-UP

When sunlight first strikes the polar ocean in spring, a cascade of life begins. Where nutrients are available, phytoplankton bloom, and then the zooplankton population grows to take advantage of the abundant food. Animals from small fish to enormous whales feast on the zooplankton, particularly krill, the organism with the greatest biomass on Earth. Some animals migrate into the polar ocean for the summer feast and then migrate out in winter to breed. Others live or breed on land but feed in the seas. The polar oceans, particularly the Southern Ocean, are extremely important to life on Earth.

PART TWO

ATMOSPHERIC POLLUTION AND THE POLAR REGIONS

The Antarctic Ozone Hole

The Antarctic suffers one serious effect of pollution more than the rest of the world. The conditions there are perfect for the formation of the **ozone hole**, which opens up each spring over Antarctica and sometimes spreads to the southernmost tips of the southern continents. That, and a much smaller hole that opens up each year over the Arctic, will be explored in this chapter.

ATMOSPHERIC OZONE

Ozone is a molecule composed of three oxygen atoms (O_3). This gas can be a **pollutant** (or contaminant) or it can be extremely beneficial, depending on its location in the Earth's atmosphere. In the troposphere, the gas acts as a harmful pollutant brought about by a chemical reaction involving tailpipe emissions and sunlight. Tropospheric ozone is the primary component of **photochemical smog**. Ozone also acts as a **greenhouse gas**, one of the atmospheric gases that are helping to increase global temperature. Ozone smog can be extremely harmful to ecosystems and human health. Tropospheric ozone is known as "bad" ozone.

Most ozone is found in the stratosphere, however. This stratospheric ozone protects life on Earth from the Sun's harmful high-energy **ultraviolet (UV) radiation**. The ozone molecule forms when the Sun's high-energy UV breaks down some diatomic oxygen (O_2) molecules to make single O-atoms (O). These O-atoms then bond with other O_2 molecules to form O_3. The reverse process also takes place in the stratosphere, as UV energy breaks apart the O_3 to make O_2 and O. The breakdown of O_3 into O_2 and O is extremely important because O_3 absorbs lethal UVC, which is the most dangerous UV radiation, in addition to much of the dangerous UVB that comes from the Sun. Under normal conditions, inputs and outputs of O_3 into the ozone layer are equal. Stratospheric ozone is concentrated in the **ozone layer**, the region of the stratosphere where the high-energy UV is broken down. Ozone in the upper atmosphere is known as "good" ozone.

Without the ozone layer, only the most primitive life forms could exist on the Earth. Too much UVB harms enzymes and some proteins in living organisms. UVB is fatal to some simple single-celled organisms—such as algae, bacteria, and protozoa—and to the outer cells of some higher organisms, such as skin cells in humans. UVB harms photosynthesizing cells that contain **chlorophyll**, a green pigment that absorbs visible light as the energy source for photosynthesis. When chlorophyll absorbs UVB, the molecule bleaches and can no longer take in light. UVB also causes DNA damage to some multicellular organisms. **Deoxyribonucleic acid (DNA)** is the means by which an organism passes genetic information from parent to offspring. All living cells in all organisms, from microbes to plants and animals, contain DNA. When the mechanism works correctly, the DNA molecule creates an identical copy of itself so that when a parent cell divides, both daughter cells receive an exact copy of the original molecule. Exposure to UVB radiation damages the DNA so that the cell cannot "read" it, and the molecule is not replicated properly. When a single-celled organism loses DNA, it either reproduces incorrectly or dies. In a multicellular organism, the loss of some cells may be compensated for, but the loss of too many of the same types of cells causes problems.

The risk of damage to cells increases with the increase in the amount of UVB entering them. Because UVB is so damaging, many organisms have evolved protective pigments. Human skin cells, for example, make brown melanin to protect against the sunburn caused by UVB (this is also known as tanning). However, skin cancer may result from too much UVB. Some terrestrial, freshwater, and marine organisms manufacture protective pigments as well. For example, the defending pigment in some lichens is bright orange and yellow.

THE ASSAULT OF CHLOROFLUOROCARBONS ON THE OZONE LAYER

In recent decades, man-made organic chemicals have brought about a decrease in stratospheric ozone. These chemicals, of which there are several types, such as CFC-11, are known as **chlorofluorocarbons (CFCs)**. They also are commonly called freon. Problems are also caused, to a lesser extent, by bromofluorocarbons (halons), methyl bromide, carbon tetrachloride, and trichloroethane (methyl chloroform).

But CFCs are the most dangerous because they are the most abundant. For decades, these nontoxic, nonflammable, and chemically nonreactive compounds were widely used because they are cheap and extremely useful as refrigerants, cleaning agents, spray-can propellants, and building blocks for insulating foams. However, in 1973, Mario Molina, a graduate student at the University of California at Irvine, calculated the effects of CFCs on the ozone layer. When his academic advisor, Sherwood Rowland, saw his work, the two men checked and rechecked it for errors but could find none. After a review by some colleagues, Molina and Rowland published their chilling findings: CFCs were rising into the Earth's stratosphere and destroying its fragile ozone shield.

Molina and Rowland discovered that the properties that make CFCs useful also make them dangerous. Because CFCs are nonreactive, they travel unaltered through the troposphere into the stratosphere. In the stratosphere, UV breaks them down into smaller components. One of these components, chlorine (Cl), then wrenches one of the O ions away from an O_3. The chlorine ion quickly releases the oxygen ion and moves on to break apart another O_3. In this way, Cl converts an O_3 into an O_2 and an O, neither of which protects the Earth from UV radiation. The Cl from only one CFC molecule can annihilate up to 100,000 ozone molecules before it is destroyed by UV.

Initially, many scientists doubted Molina and Rowland's calculations. Scientific measurements failed to find the gradual, global decline in stratospheric ozone that Molina and Rowland's calculations predicted, so the scientists assumed that somehow CFCs must break down in the troposphere. But no one anticipated that the ozone decline would be found in a specific place during a particular season. Atmospheric scientists were stunned in 1985 when members of the British Antarctic Survey (BAS) published a paper in *Nature* showing that up to 50% of the stratospheric ozone layer had disappeared over Antarctica during the previous three springs. Members of the BAS, including J.C. Farman, B.G. Gardiner, and J.D. Shanklin, had been monitoring ozone over the Antarctic since 1957. For 20 years, they had been observing a regular seasonal cycle of ozone concentration. However, in the early 1980s, they discovered that springtime ozone levels were decreasing dramatically. The thinning of the Antarctic ozone layer has since been named the Antarctic ozone hole. Mario Molina and Sherwood Rowland won the 1995 Nobel Prize in chemistry for their momentous work in this area.

THE OZONE HOLE

Atmospheric scientists wondered, "Why did the ozone hole open in Antarctica, and why in the spring?" The answers have to do with how the atmosphere circulates and the unique conditions found at the poles. Thanks to global atmospheric circulation patterns, all Earth's air passes through the polar regions. Often, this air contains CFCs and other pollutants. During the long, dark Antarctic winter, a strong wind, known as the polar vortex, circles the pole in the middle to lower stratosphere. This motion traps the frigid air over the polar area. When air temperatures get cold enough, below about −110°F (−80°C), **polar stratospheric clouds (PSCs)** form. Rather than growing from pure water droplets like other clouds, PSCs arise from a reaction between nitric acid and water ice. PSCs, shown in the photo on this page, are crucial to ozone destruction. CFCs attach to the surfaces of these droplets and then break apart, releasing molecular chlorine (Cl_2). In the spring, when the Sun's light first hits the PSCs, UV breaks the Cl_2 into chlorine ions (Cl), and the destruction of ozone

These polar stratospheric clouds (PSCs) formed over Iceland and were photographed from a NASA DC-8 jetliner. PSCs are colorful because their tiny particles of nitric acid and water diffract sunlight. (*Mark Schoeberl / GSFC / NASA*)

begins: Chlorine chews up O_3, causing the ozone hole to grow. The hole represents a loss of 40% to 70% of ozone concentrations in a vertical column. As spring progresses, the Antarctic air mass warms and begins to move northward over the southern continents—Australia, New Zealand, southern South America, and Africa. When the ozone hole shifts over these areas, UV levels rise more than 20%.

When it was discovered in 1981, the hole was only 900,000 square miles (2 million sq. km). Since then, it has continued to grow in size, although its exact dimensions vary from year to year. In 2006, ozone levels were at an all-time low for the south polar area. The 2006 hole was nearly as large as the record hole in 2000, which reached 11.4 million square miles (28 million sq. km), more than three times the size of the United States. Although the trend has been toward larger holes over time, the size each year depends on the temperature of the stratosphere because the PSCs that form in conditions of extreme cold are crucial to the formation of the ozone hole. Because the atmosphere was especially warm, the 2002 hole was uncharacteristically small.

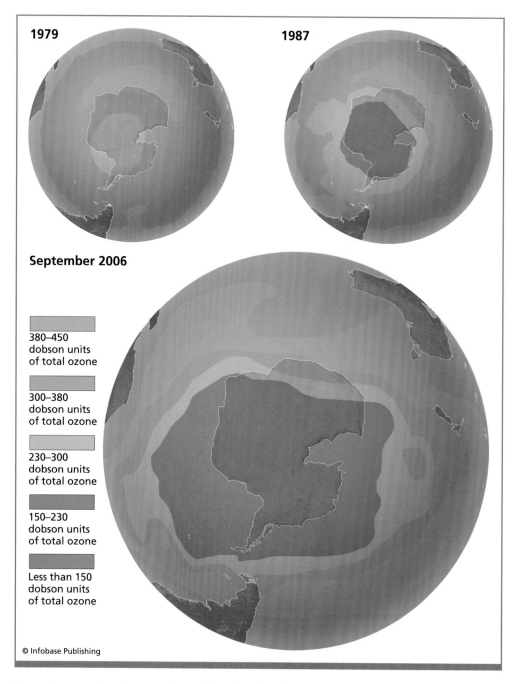

1979

1987

September 2006

380–450
dobson units
of total ozone

300–380
dobson units
of total ozone

230–300
dobson units
of total ozone

150–230
dobson units
of total ozone

Less than 150
dobson units
of total ozone

© Infobase Publishing

In 2006, ozone levels were at an all-time low for the Antarctic region. The ozone hole was nearly as large in area as the record hole in 2000, about three times the size of the United States.

The ozone hole now appears each Antarctic spring between August and early December and reaches its peak in September and early October. The total amount of ozone reduction is approximately 50%, although reductions of nearly 70% have been measured.

Ozone loss also occurs over the Arctic in the springtime, although the depletion only reaches up to 30%, which is not large enough to be called a hole. The complexity of the Arctic ground surface, with land, water, and ice, causes air to circulate more, so stratospheric temperatures do not get as cold. This results in less PSC formation and less separation of chlorine from CFCs. However, Arctic winter temperatures are extremely variable; and, in recent years, the Arctic stratosphere has grown colder and more humid, which promotes PSC formation. When this ozone-poor layer breaks up late in the spring, it moves south over the world's most populated regions—Europe, North America, and Asia. Although there is much less ozone depletion than in the Antarctic, Arctic ozone loss can affect many more people. Since 1978, UVB levels have grown about 4% per decade at 40°N, which is the latitude of New York City.

THE MONTREAL PROTOCOL

Molina and Rowland's results were serious enough to convince representatives of several countries to take action to protect the ozone layer. As early as 1978, the United States and most Scandinavian countries had banned CFCs in spray cans. Once the identification of the Antarctic ozone hole made the threat seem more real, world political leaders mobilized around an environmental issue for the first time. The **Montreal Protocol** on Substances that Deplete the Ozone Layer, an agreement that controls the production and consumption of ozone-depleting substances, was ratified in 1987, just two years after the discovery of the hole was made public, and went into force in 1989. Since then, several amendments have been signed to increase the number of controlled substances and regulate the trade of substances between developing and developed nations, all with the goal of returning the ozone layer to its 1970s area and depth.

Currently, the Montreal Protocol regulates 96 substances. The usage of most of them has not yet been banned but is being phased out. Each cutback follows two timescales: one that applies to developed countries and another for developing ones. The phase-out schedule for the developing nations is looser, with a one-decade grace period for most substances so that these nation's economic development is not hindered. The speed of the reduction also depends on a chemical's harmfulness. CFCs were phased out in the developed countries in 1995 and must be fully phased out in the developing nations by 2010.

HCFCs, which are much less ozone depleting than some of the other chemicals, are to be phased out in the developed countries using the following schedule: 35% in 2004, 65% in 2010, 90% in 2015, 99.5% in 2020, and 100% in 2030. The final 0.5% will remain available only for essential purposes. Overall, HCFCs will be frozen at 2015 levels in 2016 and will be phased out by 2040. In addition, industrialized countries were required to donate $510 million to develop technologies to aid developing nations in the move away from ozone-depleting chemicals. Compounds that are essential for the health and safety of society will continue to be produced if there is no known substitute. This provision is reviewed annually for any substance in this category.

The Montreal Protocol was the first international agreement designed to solve an important environmental problem. However, it is now feared that some of the momentum has been lost since the original agreement was ratified by 188 countries, because the 2003 amendment was ratified by only 81 countries. Nonetheless, CFC consumption has been greatly reduced: Between 1986 and 2004, CFC use dropped from 1.1 million to around 70,000 ODP tons. (ODP tons are obtained by multiplying the tons by the ozone depleting potential [ODP] of a substance relative to CFC-11.) Had use continued to climb at the pre-1980 rate, CFC consumption would have reached 3 million tons in 2010 and 8 million in 2060. By 2050, atmospheric CFC levels would have been 10 times higher than in 1980.

CFC levels in the troposphere peaked in 2000 and are now decreasing by almost 1% a year. CFCs take 10 to 20 years to travel from the lower atmosphere into the stratosphere, so stratospheric chlorine levels will continue to rise for 20 to 30 years. Also, CFCs can survive in the stratosphere for many years. These are among the reasons that the ozone hole is still getting bigger, although its rate of increase has generally declined. Other reasons for the continued growth of the ozone hole are that some substitutes for CFCs and other ozone-depleting chemicals may themselves destroy ozone, but at a lower rate. There is also a thriving black market in CFCs as developing nations sell their stocks to developed nations. Some CFC substitutes contribute to other environmental damage: For example, HCFCs and HFCs are powerful greenhouse gases.

Scientists predict that the Antarctic ozone hole may start to heal by the end of the present decade and will be healed by around 2065. The Arctic ozone hole will be healed by around 2040. Total atmospheric ozone levels will not match pre-1950 levels for another 100 to 200 years.

THE EFFECTS OF OZONE LOSS ON THE POLAR REGIONS

For many decades, the ozone hole will be a feature of the Antarctic and, to a lesser extent, the Arctic regions. The resulting increased UVB will continue to disturb polar organisms by, for example, damaging photosynthesizing cells and DNA.

Ozone loss has been shown to harm Antarctic marine organisms. A 2006 study by Andrew Davidson of the Australian Antarctic Division in Tasmania looked at the marginal ice zone where one-quarter to two-thirds of all Southern Ocean phytoplankton bloom. Davidson's team used satellite images to study the relationship of chlorophyll, which they used to represent the total number of phytoplankton, to ozone concentration. Davidson discovered that when ozone levels were low, chlorophyll levels decreased dramatically—to less than half of their value when ozone levels were high. As a result, UVB significantly reduced the phytoplankton blooms in the Southern Ocean. No one knows exactly why phytoplankton numbers drop when ozone levels are low. Scientists speculate that photosynthesizing phytoplankton may try to escape increased UVB by sinking deeper into the water. Although this decreases their UVB exposure, it also decreases their contact with visible light and lessens their ability to photosynthesize.

During times of ozone depletion, the daily food energy produced by Antarctic phytoplankton has been found to be reduced by as much as 12%. This may equal a 2% to 4% annual loss in food energy production. With less food, the phytoplankton have less energy to reproduce, and fewer phytoplankton means less food for other organisms. Scientists have calculated that a 16% depletion of ozone could result in a 5% loss of phytoplankton and the subsequent loss of 7 million tons of fish per year. When phytoplankton numbers go down, it is likely that krill numbers go down, which directly affects the marine mammals and birds that depend on them.

Animals up the food chain are also directly affected by increased UVB levels. Scientists have found that, in the laboratory, krill DNA is damaged by UVB. However, when UV levels are high, the krill themselves acquire natural sunscreens (mycosporine-like amino acids) from the algae they eat, so they appear not to be directly damaged by UVB. Antarctic icefish eggs and larvae are damaged by UVB, which slows their growth and reduces their cells' ability to repair their DNA. All of these factors could limit the animals' ability to survive into adulthood.

There have been few studies of the consequences of increased UVB on polar land areas, but those that have been conducted have shown few effects. Because tundra plants likely evolved from plants that migrated poleward, they may be preadapted to higher UV levels. The effects of UVB on polar land animals have not been well studied.

Increased human exposure to UVB has been shown to increase skin cancers and cataracts. One study showed that a 10% rise in UVB increased melanomas (the most serious type of skin cancer). Residents of Punta Arenas, Chile, at 53°S on the tip of South America, saw an increase in melanoma of 56% and in nonmelanoma skin cancer of 46% over a period of seven years as the springtime ozone hole moved over the area.

WRAP-UP

Conditions in the Antarctic are just right for the creation of the ozone hole. Prevailing air currents carry pollutants toward the South Pole, frigid air stimulates PSC formation, air stagnates during the winter, and the arrival of sunlight breaks up CFC molecules in the spring. For these reasons, stratospheric ozone loss is much greater in the Antarctic than anywhere else on Earth. Although the Antarctic ozone hole continues to grow—the lowest ozone levels were recorded in 2006—scientists expect that the ozone layer will soon begin to heal. Despite some problems, the Montreal Protocol, an international treaty that phases out the use of ozone-depleting substances, has been a singular success in the environmental movement. A similar success is necessary to protect the polar regions and the rest of the world from global warming, a topic that will be explored in the rest of Part Two.

Global Warming and the Polar Regions

Temperatures are rising worldwide and nowhere more so than in the polar regions. This phenomenon, known as **global warming**, is attributed to human activities that increase levels of greenhouse gases in the atmosphere. Carbon dioxide and **methane** (a hydrocarbon gas) are extremely important greenhouse gases because they are the most abundant and their concentrations are the most altered by human activities. The relationship of greenhouse gases and global warming to Arctic and Antarctic climates is the subject of this chapter.

GREENHOUSE GASES AND RISING TEMPERATURES

Greenhouse gases cause temperatures to rise by trapping heat in the atmosphere. When the Sun's rays enter the Earth system, they pass through the atmosphere and then strike the planet's surface. This solar energy is absorbed by soil, rock, concrete, or water and is then emitted back from the planet's surface as heat. In the atmosphere, some of this heat is trapped by greenhouse gases, a phenomenon known as the **greenhouse effect**. Without the greenhouse effect, the Earth's average atmospheric temperature would be 0°F (−18°C). Temperatures also would be extremely variable, scorching in the daytime and frigid at night, as happens on the Moon and those planets without an atmosphere. The greenhouse effect keeps the Earth's average temperature at a moderate 59°F (15°C).

Most greenhouse gases are present naturally in the environment, although a few are man-made and have only entered the atmosphere in recent decades. **Water vapor** enters the atmosphere when water evaporates. The amount of water vapor that air can hold depends on its temperature: Warm air holds more water vapor than cold air. **Carbon dioxide (CO_2)** enters the atmosphere during **respiration**, the process in which plants or animals exchange oxygen and CO_2; volcanic eruptions; and the burning of plant material. Methane, a **hydrocarbon** (hydrogen and carbon) gas, is a byproduct of decomposition and the biochemical reactions that occur in cow stomachs (for example, by cows passing gas). The **nitrous oxides**, NO and NO_2, (known together as NO_x) are produced naturally by bacterial action. Ozone is found naturally in the lower atmosphere in small amounts. These amounts are increased by the creation of photochemical smog. Chlorofluorocarbons (CFCs), which are primarily responsible for stratospheric ozone loss, are greenhouse gases that are entirely man-made.

Air pollution is made up of particles and toxic gases that are emitted by human activities and can cause damage to the environment or human health. Pollutant particles have a variety of effects on temperature. Some particles may reflect solar energy back into space, but others absorb heat and increase warming.

Of the greenhouse gases, water vapor has the greatest impact on global temperature because it is the most abundant. Water vapor in the atmosphere increases with higher air temperature; and because global warming increases atmospheric temperature, global warming also increases atmospheric water vapor levels. This is an example of a positive feedback mechanism, a phenomenon in which one action leads to a set of events that increase that same action. In this case, the positive feedback can be seen to spur global warming. By contrast, with a negative feedback mechanism, one action weakens the response to the action. One example is when higher temperatures in the atmosphere allow the air to hold more water vapor, which forms clouds that reflect back solar energy, which in turn will cause cooling.

Not all greenhouse gases have the same heat-trapping ability. For example, one CFC molecule traps as much heat as 10,000 CO_2 molecules. Methane traps about 23 times as much heat as CO_2. This means that, despite their presence in very low quantities, these particular gases have an increased impact on global warming.

Greenhouse gases are constantly being removed from the atmosphere. Gases are absorbed by water, so large amounts of CO_2 are

Arctic Haze

More than a century ago, Norwegian polar explorer Fridtjof Nansen (1861–1930) noticed inexplicable dark stains on the polar ice during one of his expeditions. According to Tim Garrett, an assistant professor and author of a 2006 University of Utah press release on the subject, "Whalers and explorers noticed what looked like pollution and couldn't figure out where it was coming from." The Inuit called it *poo-jok*. Even back then, industrial pollutants were wafting on atmospheric currents from regions far to the south and polluting the once-pristine Arctic environment.

Pilots on weather reconnaissance flights in the late 1940s described a dense haze sitting over the far north. The following decade, the pollution had a name: **Arctic haze**. The haze is made of **aerosols,** which are tiny particles of liquid or solid suspended in the air. While the aerosols in Arctic haze are pollutants, these particles can also come from natural sources. Aerosols serve as nuclei for tiny water droplets to condense around during cloud formation.

Arctic haze is caused by northward-flowing air currents that bring in pollutants from Eurasia during the winter. The aerosols stagnate in the dry, frigid air under a pronounced **inversion**, a situation in which cold air is trapped beneath warmer air. When the first springtime light arrives, the haze over the area resembles the smog over a large city. Arctic haze blankets an area roughly the size of Africa and is thickest on the Alaskan north slope. The pollutants are mostly sulfates (SO_4 compounds) contained in the oceans. Cold water holds more gas than warm water, so when water warms, the gases bubble out, back into the atmosphere. CO_2 is also stored in plant tissue. When plants die and are turned into **fossil fuels** deep in the Earth, their CO_2 is stored with them. (Fossil fuels are ancient plants that Earth processes have transformed into oil, natural gas, coal, and other materials.) In the past, the greenhouse gases stored in fossil fuels and plant tissues were kept out of the atmosphere; this prevented the planet from overheating.

Now some of this stored CO_2 is being released back into the atmosphere. Although people have been burning wood and coal to meet their energy needs for thousands of years, fossil fuel usage has

mixed with particles of carbon but contain nearly every pollutant found in the developed world, including **heavy metals**, such as mercury and lead, and the gases CO_2, methane, and carbon monoxide. (A heavy metal is a metal with high specific gravity; that is, high weight for a given volume.) The haze is not as pronounced in summer because the air is moister, and the rain is more likely to wash out the pollutants.

When the haze clears, it may spread to other portions of the northern hemisphere. In the wetter months, the pollutants may be picked up by falling rain or snow or drop out of the atmosphere onto snow, ice, or soil. Contaminants that reach the ground often end up in meltwater that feeds surface waters. Lichens accumulate pollutants for decades until they are re-

leased into the tissues of grazing animals, such as caribou, that may later be eaten by local people.

Haze also accelerates warming in the Arctic. The soot absorbs greenhouse gases in the atmosphere. Soot also decreases albedo and absorbs heat when it falls onto snow and ice, which causes more rapid melting. The water droplets that are created around aerosol pollutants are smaller and more numerous than those that form naturally. Clouds formed of these droplets reflect incoming sunlight back into space more effectively than normal clouds, but they also trap the heat that reradiates off the ground more effectively. University of Utah scientists have calculated that polluted, cloudy days are 2° to 3°F (1.1 to 1.7°C) warmer in the Arctic than clear days.

increased astronomically since the beginning of the Industrial Revolution about 150 years ago. In addition, **slash-and-burn agriculture**, a method of clearing land for growing food in the tropics, releases the CO_2 stored in rain forests and is common today.

Atmospheric CO_2 levels have been rising precipitously. The total CO_2 has increased 27% since the Industrial Revolution, from a value of 280 parts per million (ppm) to a value of 381 ppm (the highest as of June 2007). (One part per million is one part out of one million equal parts; one part per billion is one part out of one billion parts. Percent, in comparison, can be thought of as parts per hundred.) Nearly 65% of that rise has taken place since scientists began measuring CO_2 on Mauna Loa volcano in Hawaii in 1958, when the atmospheric CO_2 was 316 ppm. The rate at which CO_2 increases continues to climb. In fact, it has doubled in the past 30 years. One of the largest single-year increases on record—a rise of 2.6 ppm—occurred in 2005.

The methane content of the atmosphere is also increasing as livestock, rice production, and the incomplete burning of rain forest materials release the gas in ever higher amounts. Since the Industrial Revolution, atmospheric methane levels have risen 151%, mostly from agricultural sources. CFC levels have increased from zero in 1928, when production of the man-made chemicals began. Although CFCs are now being phased out because of their role in ozone depletion, other synthetic heat-trapping gases are still being manufactured and released into the atmosphere. Concentrations of tropospheric ozone, a pollutant and greenhouse gas, have more than doubled since 1976.

Along with atmospheric greenhouse gas levels, average global temperature has also been rising. The 1990s were the warmest decade on record and seem almost certain to be surpassed by the 2000s. The five warmest years in the past millennium through 2006 were (in descending order) 2005, 1998, 2002, 2003, and 2006; and the 13 hottest years have been since 1990. Recent scientific evidence shows that the past 10- to 20-year period was the warmest period of at least the past two millennia.

CLIMATE CHANGE IN THE POLAR REGIONS THROUGH TIME

People who are skeptical that global warming is taking place, and that it is being caused by human activities, argue that Earth's climate changes naturally and that climate has been extremely variable throughout Earth history. This is certainly true: There have been hot, wet periods, such as when the dinosaurs ruled the planet, and ice ages, when much of the surface was covered by glaciers and sea ice. The polar regions have experienced different climates just as much as other regions, or even more.

During the Paleocene-Eocene Thermal Maximum (PETM) that took place 55 million years ago, the Arctic was a vast swamp where the average temperature was a balmy 74°F (23°C). Antarctica was covered with forests. Evidence suggests that global temperatures were rising due to other causes, such as changes in the tilt of the planet relative to the Sun. As the seas warmed, they melted the vast reservoir of methane hydrates that lies beneath seafloor sediments. **Methane hydrates** are an unstable substance in which water molecules form an icy cage (a hydrate) that contains a methane molecule. When the ice melts, the methane is released into the atmosphere, where some of it converts to CO_2. The large load of methane and CO_2 that entered the atmosphere caused temperatures to rise globally. The PETM lasted for about 200,000 years, likely ending when all the susceptible methane had been released into the atmosphere and the excess atmospheric methane and CO_2 had been taken up by trees and plankton and dissolved into the oceans.

After the PETM, temperatures generally declined. Ice began to accumulate in both the Arctic and Antarctic about 14 million years ago. Conditions grew much colder approximately 1.8 million years ago when the **Pleistocene Ice Age** began. Scientists attribute the Pleistocene to variations in the Earth's tilt, which changed the amount of incoming solar energy. The Pleistocene had both glacial and interglacial periods, when the ice advanced or retreated. During glacial advances, global temperatures were about 10°F (5.5°C) colder than today. Sea level was about 395 feet (125 m) lower because so much water was trapped in the ice. During interglacial periods, global temperatures were more than 2°F (1.1°C) higher than now, and sea level was about 16 feet (4.8 m) higher. During glacial periods, atmospheric greenhouse gas levels were low, and during interglacial periods they were high, although CO_2 levels never rose above 300 ppm and were stable at or below 280 ppm for at least 400,000 years.

During the final glacial advance of 18,000 years ago, the Laurentide Ice Sheet covered North America from that latitude of present-day New York City northward. Similar ice sheets coated Eurasia and other northern regions. The remains of the last glacial advance can still be seen in the glaciers, ice caps, sea ice, permafrost, and lakes of the polar areas. Since that glacial maximum, average global temperature has risen 7°F (4°C). But the temperature has not risen at an even rate; 6°F (3.4°C) of the rise took place in the first 18,000 years, and 1.0°F (0.6°C) came about just in the past century. The Arctic is still not as warm as it was during some interglacial periods, and global climate is still within the Pleistocene glacial–interglacial range. Some scientists suggest that another glacial advance will come, but probably not for another millennium or more.

Climate has also varied in more recent time. This, at times, has had a major impact on human populations. Around A.D. 1000, during the relatively warm Medieval Warm Period (MWP), the Vikings spread across northern Europe and into Greenland and Iceland, where they grew crops, raised farm animals, and hunted. The weather turned against the thriving colonies in the fourteenth century, as Europe plunged into the Little Ice Age (LIA), and temperatures dropped between 0.9° and 1.8°F (0.5° and 1.0°C). Many Vikings abandoned Greenland, and those that remained starved to death. Using hunting methods that are well-suited to icy temperatures, the Inuit and other indigenous northerners survived the LIA in better shape.

Arctic temperatures have varied even in the past century. As shown in the graph on page 72, in the 1920s and 1930s, temperatures

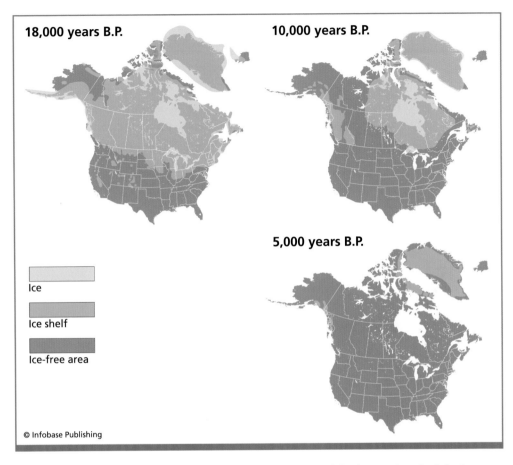

18,000 years B.P.

10,000 years B.P.

5,000 years B.P.

Ice

Ice shelf

Ice-free area

© Infobase Publishing

The extent of the North American ice sheet at the height of the last major glacial advance, 18,000 years before the present (B.P.); during the Younger Dryas, 10,000 years B.P.; and after glaciers had completely retreated from the temperate zones, 5,000 years B.P. Since the last glacial advance, glaciers have been in retreat, with minor advances due to small-scale cooling events.

in some Arctic locations were nearly as high as temperatures now. The difference is that the high temperatures of the past were regional and could be tied to natural climate variations. Natural climate variations can be caused by shifts in atmospheric and oceanic conditions due partially to the way heat is stored and transported in the oceans. An example of a relatively short-term natural climate variation is the **El Niño**, which typically alters climate for a few years. Other known natural climate variations alter climate on a scale of decades.

But now temperatures are rising throughout the entire Arctic and Antarctic and are connected to rising temperatures around the Earth. According to the climate records that scientists have created based on ice core samples and samples from ocean sediments going back many years, it is clear that temperature levels are related to greenhouse gas levels. A graph of CO_2 and temperature over the past 450,000 years (see page 73) shows this correlation. Although the relationship between the two is complicated, the result is clear: When CO_2 is high, temperatures are high; and when CO_2 is low, temperatures are low.

During most periods of climate change, greenhouse gas levels do not trigger global warming. A look at the graphs shows that during

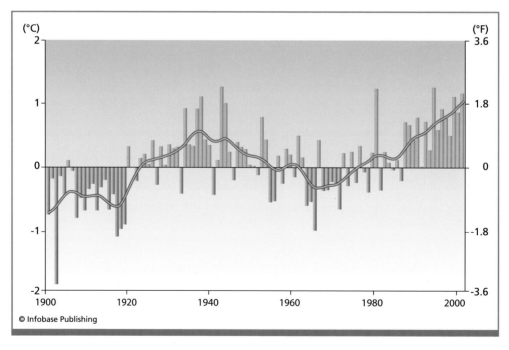

Arctic temperatures in the 20th century, from the Arctic Climate Impact Assessment. Average annual change in near-surface air temperature from stations on land is shown relative to the average, 1960 to 1990, for the region from 60°N to 90°N.

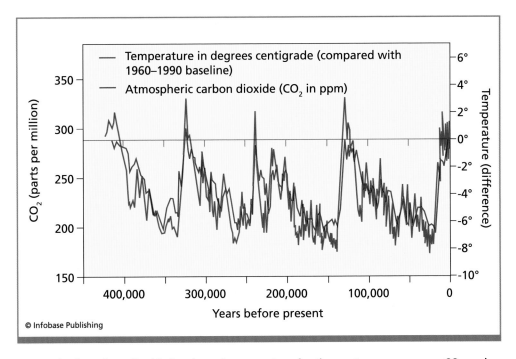

Atmospheric carbon dioxide levels and temperature for the past 450,000 years. CO_2 and temperature show the same pattern; temperature and CO_2 are high during interglacial periods and low during glacial periods. CO_2 does not drive the initial rise in temperature during an interglacial but is a major contributor after the initial temperature rise. The rise in CO_2 since 1958 has been picked up by the Mauna Loa monitoring station. In recent years, temperature increases have not kept up with CO_2.

interglacial periods, CO_2 begins to rise between 600 and 1,000 years after temperatures rise. Ordinarily, some factor, such as the Earth's tilt, initiates the climate change; and greenhouse gases provide positive feedbacks later. The PETM is a good example of this relationship.

Now it seems that greenhouse gases are the climate change trigger. Although the idea was considered controversial several years ago, nearly all climate scientists now link the accelerated temperature increase with rising atmospheric greenhouse gases due to the widespread burning of fossil fuels and plant materials. Many of the world's politicians are also now recognizing the importance of greenhouse gases and global warming. In a 2004 speech, then–British Prime Minister Tony Blair called climate change the world's greatest environmental challenge. He stated, "Our effect on the environment, and in particular on climate change, is large and growing." At this time, not all powerful world leaders agree.

CLIMATE MODELS

To determine the path of future climate change and what the effects of global warming will be, scientists construct **climate models**. Researchers input into supercomputers the data gathered from modern measurements; past climate; and current ideas on how land, atmosphere, oceans, and ice interact. A climate model can be created for a local area or for the entire globe.

When modeling climate, scientists must take many interactions into account. One is a **threshold effect**. An example of such an effect is the water-ice transition: A rise in temperature of 1.8°F (1°C) from 29.3° to 31.1°F (−1.5° to −0.5°C) will not have much effect on a local glacier. But the same magnitude of temperature increase will have an enormous effect if the rise is from 31.1° to 32.9°F (−0.5° to 0.5°C) because that temperature increase crosses the threshold for ice to melt. Polar areas are especially sensitive to warming temperatures because of the water-ice threshold. Important temperature thresholds are different for specific locations, for biological systems, and for the planet as a whole.

Feedback mechanisms, both positive and negative, are also important when modeling climate. The water-ice transition involves several positive feedbacks for global warming. For example:

- Increasing temperature reduces ice cover, which reduces albedo and increases the temperatures of the exposed land and sea.
- Warmer ocean water more easily transfers heat into the atmosphere, which increases air temperature.

- Increasing temperature reduces sea ice, which exposes more warm open water and decreases the likelihood that sea ice will form the next year.
- When sea ice forms, it is thinner and therefore more likely to melt the following summer.

Climate is a very complex system; climate models are difficult to put together. To check the validity of a new model, scientists try to reproduce events that have already occurred. If a model can accurately reconstruct conditions that existed in the past or present, scientists can use it to predict the future with some degree of confidence. Climate models are also constantly updated.

The success of a model depends in part on the scientists' ability to account for the interactions of land, atmosphere, ocean, and living things. However, some factors are not well understood. Clouds, for example, have two competing effects on climate: They reflect sunlight back into space (as can be felt when a cloud passes overhead), and they trap heat (as on a cloudy night). If warmer temperatures increase cloud cover, the effects are unclear and so are not easy to model.

Scientists cannot know how accurate models of future climate change will be until the time modeled is reached. Scientists do know, however, that the models are all pointing in the same direction, and the changes now being observed around the world have been predicted by existing climate models. These facts, along with the ability of a model to accurately predict events that have already happened, give them the conviction that the models are on the right track.

GLOBAL EFFECTS OF RISING TEMPERATURES

The effects of warmer temperatures are being seen around the globe. No one event can be attributed unequivocally to warmer temperatures, but the total of all the changes that are taking place has convinced climate scientists that human-induced global warming is happening. A table of some of the effects and where they are taking place is shown in the table on pages 76–77.

Effects of Global Warming Already Being Seen

LOCATION	EFFECT OF WARMING TEMPERATURES
Global	Precipitation patterns are changing: Wet regions are becoming wetter; dry regions are becoming drier.
	Extreme weather—heat waves, drought, floods, and hurricanes—is increasing in frequency and duration.
	Mountain glaciers all around the world are retreating; for example, the rate of retreat is 328 feet (100 m) per decade in the Andes of South America.
	Ice cover on lakes is thinner, less extensive, and present for a shorter time in winter.
	Rivers have lower water volume; peak flow comes earlier in the spring.
	Some terrestrial organisms are moving poleward or uphill to find suitable conditions.
	Life cycle events of some organisms are happening earlier in spring; for example, by an average of 2.3 days per decade for 1,700 Northern Hemisphere species studied.
	Species are migrating northward at an average of 3.8 miles (6.1 km) per decade in a study of 1,700 Northern Hemisphere species.

WRAP-UP

Scientists have developed ingenious methods for reconstructing past climate. Using these tools, they have discovered that climate has varied enormously in the Earth's past, and that greenhouse gas levels are high when temperatures are high and are low when temperatures are low. Scientists have also discovered that greenhouse gases rise

LOCATION	EFFECT OF WARMING TEMPERATURES
Arctic	Reduction in summer sea ice cover of 20% since 1979
	Greater melting from the Greenland ice sheet
	Permafrost melting
Antarctic	Collapse of Larsen A (1995) and Larsen B (2002) ice shelves
	Greater melting of the Antarctic ice sheet
Oceans	Global sea surface temperature increase of 0.9°F (0.5°C) over the past four to five decades
	Global sea level rise of 8 inches (20 cm) in the past century, increasing to 0.1 inches (0.3 cm) per year between 1993 and 2005
	Globally, 70% of sandy beaches are eroding.
	Hurricanes are increasing in intensity, distribution, and possibly frequency, causing greater amounts of damage.
	North Atlantic plankton and fish have moved northward 10° in latitude in 40 years.
	Coral reefs are bleaching and losing their ability to produce food.

in response to warming temperatures and that greenhouse gases can drive temperature changes. The increases in atmospheric greenhouse gas levels are due to human activities—primarily fossil fuel burning, but also modern agricultural practices. By constructing climate models, scientists can predict what these increasing greenhouse gas levels will do to temperatures around the world, including those in the polar regions. The effects of global warming are now being seen around the world and include changing weather, retreating glaciers and sea ice, increased storms, and the movement of land and marine organisms to higher altitudes and higher latitudes. The effects of warmer temperatures on the polar regions are described in the following chapter.

The Effects of Global Warming on the Polar Regions

Temperatures are not rising at the same rate around the globe. While a few places have cooled in the past few decades, most areas are warmer. The most extreme changes have been seen in the higher latitudes. Western Siberia, for example, has heated more than anywhere else on Earth, some 5.4°F (3°C) in the past 40 years. Over the Antarctic Peninsula, temperatures have climbed by 4.5°F (2.5°C) in the past 50 years. The effects of global warming in the polar regions include melting ice caps and glaciers, shortened winters, more extreme weather, and alterations in the timing of major life cycle events in plants and animals. The people of the Far North are witnessing changes in the Arctic that are more severe than in any other environment on Earth. These changes are the subject of this chapter.

EFFECTS OF GLOBAL WARMING ON THE ARCTIC

The effects of global warming are best seen in the Arctic. This region is responding more to rising temperature than regions elsewhere because of the way its temperatures hover around water's freezing point at certain times of the year. Also, the Arctic is much better known than the Antarctic. Indigenous people have been living in the Arctic for generations and have depended on a precise sequence of seasonal events to hunt and live in that harsh environment. By being in tune with the region's climate, they are able to report on the changes they have seen regarding the extent of ice, the weather, the duration of the seasons, and the behavior of plants and animals, among other phenomena. Much information on Arctic climate change is presented in the Arctic Climate Impact Assessment (ACIA), a 2004 report by more than 300 scientists that took over three years to produce. Some of the results of that assessment are discussed in this volume.

Many scientists say that some of the changes that have been taking place in the Arctic environment, and possibly even the entire region itself, have passed the **tipping point**. Climate reaches the tipping point when catastrophic change becomes inevitable—it is the point at which it is too late to act. Different tipping points exist for different phenomena. In the case of an ice sheet, for example, meltwater lubricates the glacier, which causes it to slide more and melt faster. A reduction in sea ice around the ice sheet's edges will allow warm seawater to eat away at the ice from the coast. Once an ice sheet goes past its tipping point, it will not stop melting and breaking up until it is gone, or until the onset of the next ice age.

Although natural and human factors are both currently influencing climate, several recent climate models suggest that within a few decades, greenhouse gas levels will be the major influence on Arctic climate, possibly for centuries. Nearly all models show that even if greenhouse gases grow only modestly, summer sea ice is likely to disappear by the end of the century, and much of it as early as 2050. Only the models in which greenhouse gas emissions are held constant at 2000 values (levels that are already too late to achieve) predict that the Arctic will be able to retain much of its summer sea ice. If the Arctic region reaches its tipping point, the end result may be a long-term change in the region's color from white to blue and green.

Glacier Loss on Land

On land, glaciers are melting back. Snowfall has increased in the interior of Greenland because warmer air carries more moisture for precipitation. But Greenland's ice mass has decreased by 50 cubic miles (208 cubic km) as the ice sheet melts and giant icebergs calve into the sea. The Greenland ice sheet is experiencing several positive feedbacks for melting that include

- warmer temperatures melting the ice sheet at its edges
- ice shelves melting back, which allows seawater to move closer in to the glacier, warming it, and causing it to melt
- meltwater traveling between the ice sheet and the underlying rock, causing the glacier to slip at its base and enter the melting zone more rapidly
- meltwater penetrating into cracks in the ice and weakening it, causing it to slide toward the sea.

Since satellite observations began in 1979, the Greenland ice sheet has melted back 16% and ice loss in Greenland is accelerating: The ice cap melted twice as fast in 2006 as in the prior five years. In early May 2006, temperatures were almost 20°F (11°C) above normal, just below freezing. As temperatures rise above the freezing point so early in the summer season, more melting takes place. This may greatly hasten the loss of the Greenland ice sheet.

Alaska's mountain glaciers are also receding. Portage Glacier, located about 65 miles (105 km) south of Anchorage, is retreating at a rate of about 165 feet (50 m) a year. Muir Glacier in Glacier Bay National Park has retreated more than 5 miles (8 km) in the last 30 years. The warmest summers ever recorded in human history have dried out the trees and soil and made forests more vulnerable to forest fires.

Greenland Ice Sheet Melt, 1992 to 2002

1992

2002

© Infobase Publishing

The locations where ice was melting on Greenland in 2002 were much more extensive than where ice was melting in 1992.

Reduction in Permafrost

The permafrost is shrinking in many parts of the Arctic. Scientists have evidence that since 1899 the southern extent of permafrost in the Canadian Yukon has moved north 60 miles (100 km), although accurate records go back only 30 years. Permafrost around the Arctic has been thawing at an increased rate since the early 2000s. Arctic permafrost may be beginning to melt uncontrollably, and researchers are discovering that the frozen fields of peat are becoming a land of mud and lakes.

The melting of permafrost has many serious consequences. Frozen lands are more stable than loose soils, and the loss of permafrost intensifies the removal and transport of sediments from their original location by wind, ice, or gravity, a process known as **erosion**. These effects coupled with higher seas are swamping some native Alaskan villages. Lost permafrost also causes soil layers to collapse, changing the contour of the land surface and damaging the infrastructure that people rely on to work and live in the Arctic. Oil companies, for example, find it difficult to maintain and drive on roads in the far north as permafrost deteriorates. The number of days in which oil companies can explore for oil on Alaska's North Slope has already been cut in half in 30 years. In addition, highways buckle, buildings destabilize, structures collapse, and trees lean at crazy angles, a phenomenon called *drunken forests*.

Where the melting is extreme, lands that were frozen for thousands of years turn into **wetlands**, poorly drained landscapes that are covered all or a large portion of the year with water. Soggy lands are unstable environments for animals to move around on, and permafrost loss threatens the migrations of animals such as caribou. (However, new ponds and lakes may form in thawed spots where the surface sinks, creating more aquatic habitat.)

Thawing permafrost is a positive feedback for global warming. Permafrost contains peat—decayed and partially decayed plants that contain both CO_2 and methane. When frozen peat defrosts, those greenhouse gases are released into the atmosphere. Permafrost in some areas contains methane hydrates that will also melt as temperatures warm.

"There's a lot of carbon stored in the soil," says David Lawrence of the National Center for Atmospheric Research (NCAR) in Boulder, Colorado, in a December 2005 press release. "If the permafrost does thaw, as our model predicts, it could have a major influence on climate."

Climate scientists are especially concerned about Siberia, which is a frozen peat bog the size of France and Germany that harbors permafrost known as yedoma permafrost. As the ancient dead plants defrost, they are decomposed by microbes. Methane, the byproduct of this decomposition, is bubbling out of Siberian lakes, adding the gas to the atmosphere at five times the rate previously suspected, according to a study authored by Katey Walter of the University of Alaska, Fairbanks, published in *Nature* in 2006. Walter's study increases the estimate of methane emissions into the atmosphere from northern wetlands by between 10% and 63%, an amount that must now be included in climate models.

"Permafrost models predict significant thaw of permafrost during this century, which means that yedoma permafrost is like a time bomb waiting to go off—as it continues to thaw, tens of thousands of teragrams of methane can be released to the atmosphere enhancing climate warming," Walter stated in a 2006 press release.

Computer simulations from the NCAR, published in December 2005, looked at the fate of shallow Arctic permafrost within the top 11 feet (3.4 m) of the surface. Using a model that assumed that greenhouse gas emissions would continue to rise on the same trajectory they have been on for the past decade, scientists calculated that over half of the permafrost could thaw by 2050 and up to 90% of it by 2100. Using a more conservative model, in which emissions are reduced by conservation and alternative energy, it was predicted that Arctic permafrost would still shrink to less than half its current extent by the end of the century.

The Arctic Ocean

Each year, the Arctic ice cap grows in the winter and shrinks in the summer. Since 1979, when scientists first used satellites to monitor the extent of sea ice in September, they have witnessed an enormous increase in summertime ice loss. In September 2007, satellites revealed the largest retreat of sea ice recorded up through that date, with more open water than had ever been measured and probably with more than had appeared in the past 100 years. This loss of about 40% beyond the 1979 to 2000 average shattered the previous record from September 2005. The difference equals 460,000 square miles (1.19 million sq. km), roughly the size of California and Texas combined.

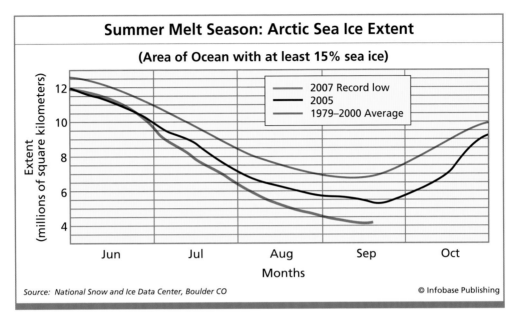

Arctic summertime sea ice extent in 2005 and 2007 compared with the average from 1979 to 2000. The past several years have seen a large decrease in sea ice even relative to that recent time period, with 2007 being the record low as of September 2007.

The growth of wintertime sea ice has also decreased since 1979, by 1.5% per decade. In March 2006, winter sea ice extent was the lowest ever measured, a record narrowly missed in March 2007.

Some scientists say that part of the loss in sea ice is due to natural variations in wind patterns. These winds are causing the Arctic ice cap to revolve around the Arctic Ocean like a giant turntable, allowing ice to flow south in the North Atlantic past Greenland. However, scientists disagree on how much of the sea ice loss is due to this natural phenomenon. Scientists do say that the dramatic loss seen in 2007 can only be explained if human-caused warming is added to the climate models.

The reduction in sea ice extent is affecting Arctic ecosystems. Plankton that live beneath the sea ice are not breeding in as high numbers, which reduces food for organisms higher up the food web. Sea ice loss also destroys the habitat polar bears need to survive. At the southern edge of these animals' ranges, the ice melts earlier in the spring, so the bears have less time to hunt. The result is that body weight of polar bears living in some locations has dropped about 22%, and they also produce fewer healthy cubs. Some reports say that polar bear populations are increasing, but NASA scientist Claire Parkinson, who studies the bears, says the opposite is true. Parkinson's 2006 study shows that with more open water, the bears are moving onto land, where they are more easily spotted, as shown in the photo on this page. In the Hudson Bay of Canada, the bear population has dropped from 1,200 in 1989 to 950 in 2004. Recently, increasing numbers of polar

Alaskan polar bear foraging for food. Increasing numbers of polar bears are being seen in towns because their sea ice hunting platforms break up early, leaving the bears hungry. (© *Gary Braasch, from the book* Earth Under Fire: How Global Warming Is Changing the World, *University of California Press, 2007.)*

bears have been reported to have drowned because they are unable to swim the increased distances between ice floes.

The World Conservation Union (IUCN; formerly the International Union for the Protection of Nature, or IUPN) suggests that polar bear populations will decrease by 30% by 2050. This organization lists the species as threatened due to the warming climate. In 2003, scientists from the University of Alberta, Canada, cautioned that polar bears could be extinct in the wild by the end of the century. University professor Dr. Andrew Derocher, who studies how polar bears adapt to changing conditions, said in a press release, "The climate predictions coming out are showing massive changes in sea-ice distribution. You don't have to be a polar scientist to see that if you take away all the sea ice, you don't have polar bears any more."

Like polar bears, walrus populations are declining due to the loss of sea ice. Walrus hunt from broken ice floes. When the ice breaks up too early and the floes drift far apart, mothers out hunting become separated from their pups. An Arctic Ocean research cruise in 2004 documented for the first time lone walrus calves swimming far from shore. Because pups are dependent on mother's milk for up to two years, the nine calves that the scientists spotted likely drowned or starved. Walrus adults can become stranded on ice floes, as well.

The types of changes that warmer temperatures are predicted to bring to the Arctic Ocean organisms are now being seen in the Bering Sea, which is extremely rich in wildlife. The northern Bering Sea's Arctic climate is now transitioning to a subarctic climate. Observations by satellites, scientists in the field, and the native Yupik people indicate that seawater temperatures are increasing as sea ice cover is decreasing. A March 2006 report in *Science* by Jacqueline M. Grebmeier and others studied the ecological changes that are taking place in response to rising temperatures and declining sea ice in the region.

Much of the ecosystem is supported by bottom-dwelling invertebrates, which are especially abundant in this portion of the sea. The northern Bering Sea has a large population of sea ducks, such as spectacled eiders (*Somateria fischeri*); gray whales; bearded seals;

and walrus, all of which eat small bottom-dwelling invertebrates. Warmer bottom waters and a lessening of sea ice quality, where the ice is broken and thin rather than being part of ice floes, is causing a decline in the abundance of prey. Fish and larger invertebrates from the southern Bering Sea are moving north to eat the bottom-dwellers. Pollock are appearing in larger numbers in the northern Bering Sea, and it appears that their predators, juvenile pink salmon, are following them and colonizing rivers further north than usual. Gray whales are also moving their range northward. Spectacled eiders are declining in numbers. Similar changes occurred after 1977 when bottom temperatures warmed in the southeastern Bering Sea.

In the Arctic Ocean's frigid Canada Basin, many creatures never seen there before have recently been spotted. These include species of squid and the first known octopus. It is likely that these species are coming in with warmer waters from the south.

Arctic People

Global warming is changing conditions for indigenous and transplanted Arctic people. Warmer temperatures have caused the Inuit to have trouble following their traditional or modified-traditional ways. The weather is now more unpredictable than in times past, with stronger and more frequent winds, greater temperature extremes, and increased summer precipitation. Unpredictable weather makes hunting and fishing more dangerous because winds can strand a hunter on the ice, and hunting parties become lost in storms. Winter hunting and fishing season has been reduced by weeks now that the ice arrives later and leaves earlier each year. Although Inuit are masters at judging ice conditions, the ice has been so thin recently that hunters and fishers have accidentally fallen through. More than a dozen hunters and fishers were lost this way in 2006. Changes in ice floes also change conditions for Inuit prey species; and over the past decade, Inuit hunters have reported decreases in the number and range of mammals, particularly seals. In recent years, the Inuit have traveled by snowmobile to hunt land animals or to visit relatives, but now that the snow has become too wet and the ice too weak, snowmobile travel is more difficult. Summer hunters are cut off from the migrating caribou herds by melting ice, and for the past few years the people have not been able to reach the nesting grounds of eider ducks, which they harvest for meat, eggs, and the soft feathers they use to make clothing. When parts of northern Canada reached 87°F (31°C) in August 2006, some Inuit communities ordered air-conditioning units for the first time ever.

"What is at stake here is not just the extinction of animals but the extinction of Inuit as a hunting culture," said the leader of the Inuit Circumpolar Conference, Sheila Watt Cloutier, in a 2005 press release. "Climate change in the Arctic is a human issue, a family issue, a community issue and an issue of cultural survival."

Changes in the snow properties mean that Inuit igloos are structurally weaker. Rising seas and melting permafrost are causing some remote Alaskan fishing villages to erode away. Three villages—Kivalina, Newtok, and Shishmaref, on Alaska's western coast—will disappear within 15 years if nothing is done to protect them, according to an April 2006 report by the United States Army Corps of Engineers. In the summer of 2006, the people of Shishmaref voted to move the village at a projected cost of $100 million. At Kivalina, built on a thin barrier island 642 miles (1,030 km) northwest of Anchorage, a 40 foot (12 m) wide wall was put up for under $3 million. However, the wall protected the village from only one moderately sized storm and was damaged, so the village is looking for a new location site. Villages in other Arctic locations are suffering as well. Bykovsky, on Russia's northeast coast, is losing land at a rate of 15 to 18 feet (4.6 to 5.5 m) a year, which will ultimately wash away the small town, house by house.

In Russia, melting permafrost threatens the industrial cities built by the former Soviet Union to exploit Arctic resources. Buildings have been abandoned as unsafe as walls and foundations have cracked. In one Russian city at the edge of the permafrost boundary, 80% of buildings show signs of damage due to permafrost melting. The ground beneath the foundations of homes, airport runways, roads, and harbors is collapsing.

EFFECTS OF GLOBAL WARMING ON THE ANTARCTIC

In a March 2006 press release, scientists at the British Antarctic Survey (BAS) reported that the "Antarctic has the same 'global warming' signature as that seen across the whole Earth, but is three times larger than that observed globally." Their conclusion was based on 30 years of weather balloon measurements from over the continent.

However, temperature changes over the Antarctic are not as obvious as those of the Arctic. One reason the effects of rising temperature are less visible than those reported over the Arctic is that fewer people live in the Antarctic. No indigenous people exist to make long-term comparisons, and the scientists are restricted to working in a few areas. Antarctica is much colder than the Arctic, so a few degrees' rise in temperature does not push the ice across its melting threshold. Because Antarctica is mostly ice covered, with little tundra, few lakes and a lower diversity of animal species, not as many environments exist for observing environmental changes. However, the effects of rising temperatures are being seen around the coasts and especially on the Antarctic Peninsula.

Temperatures on the Antarctic Peninsula have really climbed: nearly 4.5°F (3°C) in the past 50 years, about 10 times the global rate. Ice shelves along the Antarctic Peninsula are collapsing, an effect of rising temperatures that just a few years ago scientists thought would not occur for many years. The largest collapse took place in 2002 when a chunk of ice the size of Rhode Island (1,255 square miles [3250 sq. km] and 650 feet [200 m] thick) known as the Larsen B ice shelf broke off. The Larsen B collapse followed the collapse of the Wilkins ice shelf in 1998 and the Larsen A ice shelf in 1995. The breakup of the Larsen B ice shelf released thousands of icebergs out into the Weddell Sea.

Using over 2,000 aerial photographs, scientists discovered that 87% of the Antarctic Peninsula's land glaciers are retreating, a phenomenon that is advancing over time from the northernmost part of the peninsula to the south. Three peninsula glaciers increased their meltwater discharge eightfold from 2000 to 2003. Ice on the peninsula is thinning at the rate of tens of feet (m) per year, and the height of some glaciers has dropped by as much as 124 feet (38 m) in six months.

Ice breaking up off of Antarctica. (© *Gary Braasch, from the book* Earth Under Fire: How Global Warming Is Changing the World, *University of California Press, 2007*)

Glaciers are also retreating around coastal Antarctica. Although this effect is still small, the rate is beginning to accelerate. For example, recent observations show that the Amundsen Sea sector of the West Antarctic ice sheet is thinning. At least two glaciers in the East Antarctic are also thinning. Where these glaciers are on bedrock that lies below sea level, their melting will cause sea level to rise.

As in the Arctic, Antarctic sea ice is melting. Krill feed on algae that live beneath the sea ice, so it is likely that this melting reduces both krill populations. Declining krill populations will ultimately reduce the populations of the animals that eat krill, including icefish, penguins, seals, whales, and many other organisms.

Penguins are also being affected by the reductions in sea ice. The Antarctic Peninsula population of Adélie penguins appears to have declined by about 50% in recent times, with whole colonies dying out. Adélie penguins do well in cold years, when there is ample sea ice and therefore krill; but in warm years, when krill are scarce, few of the young penguins survive to adulthood.

Giant icebergs that break off from ice shelves are causing problems in the Antarctic ecosystem. Enormous icebergs block sunlight from entering the water, which keeps phytoplankton from photosynthesizing. This can reduce the productivity of the Antarctic food web. Icebergs also cause problems for penguins. With increasing frequency, ice shelves that have broken off the Antarctic Peninsula are floating onto coastlines and blocking adult Emperor and Adélie penguins' route to the sea. If the female penguins cannot make it to the sea to feed and then get back to their nesting grounds in decent time, the males will abandon their eggs so that they can go feed. If the males also cannot reach the sea, the entire population may be lost.

WRAP-UP

The effects of rising temperatures are being seen throughout the polar environment. Ice is melting from glaciers, permafrost, and sea ice. Changes in their environment are causing organisms to respond: Some of them are moving to more favorable ranges, and some populations are in trouble. Some scientists fear that the processes that are under way in both the Arctic and Antarctic are reaching their tipping points, and that the emissions people are producing today will cause these regions to become unrecognizable over the next centuries. The changes that human civilization will see in the Arctic and Antarctic in the future are discussed in the next chapter.

Future Polar Climate

Because climate models show that the changes now taking place in the polar regions will far exceed those that will take place in lower latitudes, people can expect that what they are seeing now is just the proverbial "tip of the iceberg." Climate scientists agree that the Arctic of the 2100s will not resemble the Arctic people have known for the past several centuries. Organisms that are specialized for the polar environment will become extinct or greatly reduced in numbers, and the ways of life of native people will become less viable. Rising temperatures will seriously damage the infrastructure of modern life.

PREDICTING FUTURE CLIMATE

Large changes in polar environmental conditions are likely to intensify as temperatures continue to rise. Climate scientists are creating models to predict the changes that are in store, and these models indicate that the pattern of greater warming and greater environmental changes occurring in the Arctic and Antarctic will continue. "The Arctic

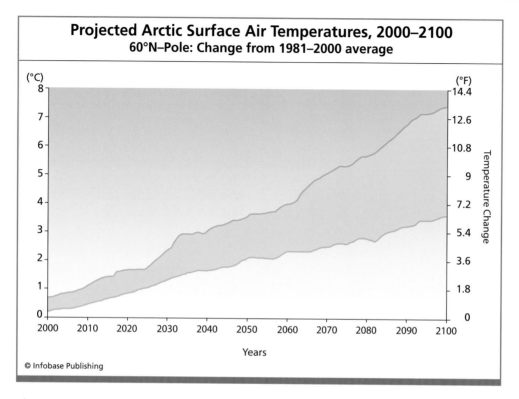

Projected Arctic Surface Air Temperatures, 2000–2100
60°N–Pole: Change from 1981–2000 average

© Infobase Publishing

The range of temperature rise in the Arctic that is predicted by various models over the 21st century, from the Arctic Climate Impact Assessment, 2004.

represents the front line of climate change and is projected to warm at a rate at least double that of the Earth as a whole," stated University of Utah Meteorology chair Jim Steenburgh in a 2006 press release.

As stated previously, modeling future climate has many uncertainties. The most important of these uncertainties is human behavior. Scientists cannot predict, for example, how much carbon people will release into the atmosphere in the coming years. Will CO_2 emissions increase at the same rate they have for the past decade, increase at an even higher rate due to improvements in lifestyles in the developing world and further improvements in the developed world, or decrease due to conscious changes in lifestyle and technology? How will the emissions of other greenhouse gases compare?

Because human behavior is unpredictable, scientists construct models using different estimates for emissions, ranging from conservative to extreme. Scientists build a large reduction in greenhouse gas emissions into a conservative model and allow emissions to grow rapidly in an extreme model. The results of these two model types are obviously very different. A comparison of both models shows a predicted average global temperature increase ranging from 0.9° to 8°F (0.5° to 4.5°C) by the end of the twenty-first century. Temperature increases will continue to affect some regions more than others. A global average temperature increase of 5°F (2.8°C) is predicted to equal 1 or 2 degrees Fahrenheit (0.6 to 1.1°C) at the equator but become as much as 12°F (6.7°C) at the North Pole.

POLAR FUTURE

A 2005 report by Jonathan Overpeck and others entitled "Arctic System on Trajectory to New, Seasonally Ice-Free State" concludes that the future of the Arctic is bleak. By the end of the century, the tundra will have retreated, most sea ice will disappear in late summer, coastlines will be eroded by higher seas, permafrost will become wetlands, and lakes atop the permafrost will drain downward as the icy bottom melts out. The report says, "There seem to be few, if any, processes or feedbacks within the Arctic system that are capable of altering the trajectory."

These authors suggest that prompt cuts in greenhouse gas emissions could keep the Greenland ice sheet from reaching its tipping point, which would prevent sea level from rising catastrophically. Of course, no one can know what the tipping point for the Greenland ice sheet is, so no one knows at what levels greenhouse gas levels need to be frozen. Many scientists think that level may be a regional increase of 5°F (2.7°C), which will correspond to a rise of 2.7°F (1.5°C) above present average global temperatures. This magnitude of global temperature increase could come with a doubling of CO_2 over pre-industrial levels (to 560 ppm), a value that could be reached as early as 2080 or even sooner. Melting of the Greenland ice sheet would take place over a long period of time, and sea level would rise over centuries or millennia.

After the tipping point for the Greenland ice sheet is reached, the ice will inevitably melt, but its large volume will keep it from melting too rapidly. Scientists had talked of Greenland's melting as taking place over millennia, but new studies have led them now to think in terms of centuries. Eventually, if the ice sheet melts completely, sea level will rise about 23 feet (7 m). The melting of Greenland could change the ocean currents and lead to a repeat of the Little Ice Age in

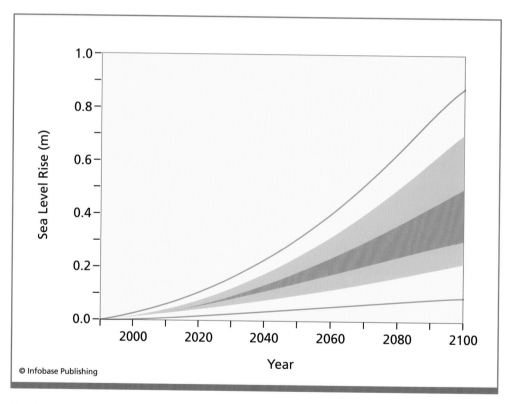

© Infobase Publishing

Sea level rise predictions for the 21st century. Just as different models of climate change predict different temperatures by 2100, they predict different amounts of sea level rise. The area with the darkest shading in the center represents model averages; the lighter green introduces more uncertainty in ice-land interactions and thermal expansion of seawater; and the bright green lines envelope possible sea level rise taking all uncertainties into account except possible changes in the West Antarctic ice sheet.

Europe as freshwater spreads over the North Atlantic Ocean, stopping or reducing the Gulf Stream current that now warms Western Europe. Similar changes in ocean currents due to large influxes of freshwater in the past took place in as little as a decade or less.

Models suggest that Antarctic ice sheets are more stable because they are larger and thicker than Greenland's. Nonetheless, the West Antarctic Ice Sheet (WAIS) is in the early stages of disintegrating, according to Chris Rapley, the head of the British Antarctic Survey (BAS). These new observations prompted Rapley to state in a 2006 press release, "Only five years ago, Antarctica was characterized as a slumbering giant in terms of climate change. I would argue that this is now an awakened giant and we should take notice." The total collapse of the West Antarctic Ice Sheet could raise sea level 16 feet (4.9 m).

The effect of the melting Greenland and WAIS ice sheets, coupled with thermal expansion due to warming ocean temperatures, would be an enormous sea level rise. In **thermal expansion**, warmer temperatures cause the water molecules to vibrate more vigorously and take up more space, resulting in a change in ocean volume. Although this effect is small, thermal expansion can result in a significant sea level rise on an oceanwide scale. The record of the geologic past suggests that during ice sheet collapse, sea level can rise 16 feet (5 m) per century. When average global temperatures were last 5°F (2.8°C) higher than today, and high latitude temperatures were 10°F (5.6°C) higher than today, sea level was 80 feet (24 m) above current sea level. This was about 3 million years ago.

Water easily absorbs CO_2. Because of this, increased CO_2 in the atmosphere has caused the oceans to absorb more of the gas. The addition of CO_2 to seawater creates carbonic acid and results in ocean **acidification**. Acidic waters decrease the ability of organisms to make carbonate shells and cause existing carbonate shells to dissolve. The effects of ocean acidification will first be seen in the polar regions because cold water absorbs CO_2 gas more readily than warmer water. If the acidity of the oceans becomes too great, phytoplankton populations could decline and initiate a collapse of ocean ecosystems. Some scientists predict that larger organisms, such as snails and sea stars, could

Andrew Revkin: *Interpreting Climate Science for a Lay Audience*

As a boy, Andrew Revkin loved nature, adventure, and writing. As a man, Revkin has brought his passions together by writing about the environment, currently for *The New York Times*. His major stories have included the 2004 Asian tsunami, the flooding of New Orleans after Hurricane Katrina, deforestation in the Amazon, the relationship of science and politics, species extinction, and climate change. In these topics, Revkin finds adventure. To follow these stories, he has traveled from the forests of the Amazon to the sea ice of the North Pole, and to many other locales. He sometimes accompanies his prose with video and photographs that he shoots himself.

Revkin has traveled to the Arctic three times to chronicle the changes taking place due to warming temperatures. His most amazing Arctic experience was a three-day journey to the North Pole in 2003, accompanying a group of scientists who are conducting an ongoing project studying the extent of sea ice melting. Because their observatory sits on floating ice, each year the researchers must dive into a hole in the ice to collect the instruments they set out the previous year, along with their data, and to deploy a new set of instruments.

Revkin strongly believes that human activities taking place very far away are having a tremendous effect on this region. "Once I got focused on the Far North,

I became fascinated by the history of exploration and science there," he said in an April 2006 interview with his publisher Houghton Mifflin/Kingfisher. "So many people died trying to conquer and comprehend this ice-cloaked ocean. It became clear that the transformation of the Arctic climate was not just a science story, but an epic shift in how we think about the planet. It was astonishing to realize that later in this century Earth could have one blue pole at some times of the year. Throughout human history both poles have been frozen whiteness."

Revkin works to inform young people about climate change because they are the ones who will be most affected by the decisions society makes now. In fact, his book about his experiences in the far north, *The North Pole Was Here*, was aimed at young audiences. The title has two meanings: Since the ice is always moving, the part of the ice that passes over the North Pole today will not be at the pole tomorrow. The other is that the North Pole as we know it will not be here in the not-so-distant future. The title, said Revkin in a 2006 interview with *Earth and Sky*, is "much more profoundly conveying that the Arctic of our history and legend, and imagination is going away. It's truly going [to be] history at this point. The North Pole was here. At least the pole that we always knew."

face trouble forming their shells in Southern Ocean surface waters as soon as 2050. Acidification could spread to other oceans by 2100.

ADAPTATION TO CLIMATE CHANGE

To maintain a semblance of their traditional way of life, Arctic people will need to adapt to changes in their environment. Inuit hunters and fishers are already making small changes by carrying extra supplies in case they become stranded by harsh conditions. Narwhal hunters pack small boats on their sleds to avoid being stranded on drifting ice. Technologies such as the Global Positional System (GPS) can tell hunters if the ice they are on is moving too far from shore, VHF radios keep them in contact with potential rescuers, and satellite images show them which icy areas to avoid.

Warming temperatures may seriously reduce the access native people have to traditional foods, so flexibility will be important. For example, in the ocean south and west of Greenland, warmer waters have caused seals to move northward. At the same time, cod, halibut, and shrimp have moved into the area, giving the native people access to a thriving cod fishery. The hunting and fishing seasons will sometimes be pushed forward or backward. Because the ice comes later in the fall, the people fish late into the summer and also begin hunting later.

When changes become too difficult to overcome, Arctic people may need to leave their native villages and move inland or to areas where the infrastructure is protected from environmental changes. According to the Arctic Climate Impact Assessment, "For Inuit, warming is likely to disrupt or even destroy their hunting and food-sharing culture as reduced sea ice causes the animals on which they depend to decline, become less accessible, and possibly become extinct."

WRAP-UP

The Arctic of the future will be very different from the Arctic that has inspired explorers, tourists, and artists for the past few centuries. Without drastic, and almost immediate, major cuts in greenhouse gas emissions, the Arctic Ocean will be nearly ice free in the summertime and will have much less winter ice cover several decades from now. The region will become warmer and swampier. Unique polar animals such as polar bears and walrus will become extinct or will survive in small pockets of surviving habitat. Northern people will be unable to continue their traditional ways and will need to find new ways of living. Even modern infrastructure will be lost. The Antarctic is on the same trajectory, but because this region is colder, and the ice is much thicker, the timescale is much different.

How far these changes go will depend on the level at which atmospheric greenhouse gases stabilize. If atmospheric temperatures rise so high that the Greenland or Antarctic ice sheets reach their tipping point, a catastrophic rise in sea level may result. Even some ice sheet melting will raise sea level and put some coastal cities in danger, especially from storms.

Tackling Global Warming

Despite the warnings about the effects that global warming will have on the polar regions, particularly the Arctic, little action is currently being taken to limit greenhouse gas emissions. This chapter will discuss how, for progress to happen, treaties will need to be negotiated and implemented to limit emissions, and technologies will need to be developed to help countries meet their greenhouse gas reduction targets. Meanwhile, individuals can make a difference by being conscious of their consumption of energy and products.

THE KYOTO PROTOCOL

The state of the polar regions stands as a warning to the rest of the world that human civilization must make reductions in its greenhouse gas emissions. Yet few nations are reducing their own emissions, and worldwide energy use and emissions are rising: The world's energy demand is projected to be 3.5 times greater in 2025 than it was in

2005. Global annual CO_2 emissions will be nearly 50% higher in 2010 than they were in 1990.

The **Kyoto Protocol** is the world's first attempt to lower greenhouse gas emissions. Like the Montreal Protocol, it seeks to solve an environmental problem by having the countries of the world agree to limit the production of environmentally damaging compounds. Kyoto was ratified in 2004 after several years of debates. Of the 130 countries that signed the treaty, 36 were industrialized nations that agreed to cut back their CO_2 emissions to at least 5% below 1990 levels by 2012.

The Inuit Versus the United States

The Inuit of the Arctic region are among the groups of people around the world who are already experiencing tremendous environmental changes due to warming temperatures. In December 2005, the leaders of the Inuit Circumpolar Conference, a group of 155,000 Inuit, filed a petition with the Inter-American Commission on Human Rights seeking a ruling that greenhouse gas emissions from the United States are violating the human rights of the Inuit and threatening their right to exist. The petition asks the Commission to declare the United States in violation of rights affirmed in the 1948 American Declaration of the Rights and Duties of Man and other instruments of international law. The petition concludes with a call for the United States to immediately reduce its greenhouse gas emissions.

Although the commission has no enforcement power, the petition asks that the commission do the following: Investigate the damage being done to the Inuit by global warming; recommend that the United States cooperate with the international community and adopt mandatory greenhouse gases emissions limits; and encourage the United States to help the Inuit develop a plan for adapting to the impacts of climate change that are already inevitable.

The leader of the Inuit Circumpolar Conference, Sheila Watt-Cloutier, spoke during a press conference in December 2005, announcing the filing of the petition. "This petition is about encouraging the United States of America to join the world community to agree to deep cuts in greenhouse gas emissions needed to protect the Arctic environment and Inuit culture and, ultimately, the world," she said. "We must never forget that, ultimately, climate change is a matter of human rights."

Unfortunately, Kyoto has many flaws, the most glaring being the countries that are not bound by it. The United States—which has only 5% of the world's population but emits the most greenhouse gases of any nation, 21% of the total in 2000—refused to sign and has agreed to engage in only voluntary cutbacks. The second largest emitter, China, released 15% of emissions in 2000; yet it, and other developing nations, are exempt in order to protect their growing economies.

Scientists predict that the emissions from the developing world will exceed those of the developed world in several decades. China's emissions are growing so rapidly that the nation is predicted to overtake the United States as the largest contributor to greenhouse gas emissions by the end of this decade. Exempting these nations from the treaty is ignoring an enormous source of greenhouse gases. Many of the nations that are bound by Kyoto, most importantly the European countries, are having trouble meeting their emissions reductions goals. Many climate scientists say that even at its best, Kyoto does not do enough to reduce greenhouse gas emissions. One climate model shows that more than 40 times the emissions reductions required by the Kyoto Protocol would be needed to prevent atmospheric CO_2 concentrations from doubling during this century.

The lack of an effective global response to rising temperatures has caused some local and regional governments, organizations, and individuals to make changes on the local level. States, cities, student organizations, and others have adopted Kyoto-like limits on greenhouse gases emissions and are working to meet those limits. While these are important, they are only the first steps in tackling what is a crucial global problem.

BEYOND KYOTO

Treaties set emissions limits, but there are further changes that governments and other organizations can make in policy and technology to help nations meet their limits. The first and easiest step is to increase energy efficiency. For example, the United States government could rapidly increase fuel economy standards for its enormous vehicle fleet to 40 mpg (17 km per liter) and require increased energy efficiency in government buildings. Requiring improved fuel efficiency in such a large market would provide enormous incentive for vehicle manufacturers and many other industries to develop more energy-efficient products. The mass production of more fuel-efficient products would result in improvements in technology and would make the products available at competitive prices for individual consumers. A **carbon tax** added to the pump price of gasoline or onto the electrical bill for households and businesses would encourage people to be more energy efficient by driving less, purchasing fuel-efficient vehicles, buying energy-efficient appliances, and keeping the heat turned down and the air-conditioning off whenever possible. The money collected could be invested in projects such as research on alternative fuels and the development of mass transit systems.

Climate scientists suggest that the second step in tackling global warming would be to move away from an economy based on the use of fossil fuels, the **carbon economy**, to an economy based on **sustainable** energy sources, which are those that can be used without compromising the needs of future generations. This would mean improvement and expansion of zero carbon energy sources such as solar, hydro, wind, geothermal, and biofuels. (Some scientists, and even some environmentalists, are recommending a resurgence in the use of nuclear power, but this is controversial due to other problems with the technology, including the disposal of nuclear waste.) Hydrogen fuel cells and coal gasification technologies are further away from being functional, but may be available in the long term.

Greenhouse gas emissions can also be sequestered after they have been created. Carbon is naturally sequestered in forests, for example, by reforesting on a large scale. Unfortunately, the amount of forest cover on the planet is declining, which contributes to greenhouse warming. Carbon can also be captured and stored in a safe place, a process known as **carbon sequestration**. Although this process is in its early stages of development, a few projects are under way. One promising sequestration method is to inject CO_2 into salt layers or coal seams so it cannot escape to the surface and into the atmosphere.

WHAT INDIVIDUALS CAN DO

There is no doubt that a unified, global response is needed to battle global warming; but meanwhile, individuals can make some difference by making good choices in how they live and how they use energy. Some valuable actions individuals can take are

- Buy only fuel-efficient vehicles. Every gallon of gasoline burned emits 20 pounds of CO_2 and many other pollutants.
- Try to live near work, school, and other activities to reduce the amount of driving.
- Reduce gasoline consumption by carpooling, taking mass transit, walking, or riding a bike.
- Buy energy-efficient appliances that have the Environmental Protection Agency's (EPA) Energy Star label.
- Determine ways in which every member of the family can reduce energy use. Even small changes can help: Boil only the amount of water needed; turn off TVs, computers, and lights when not in use; take showers instead of baths.
- Plant a tree (or two) to absorb CO_2 emissions.
- Reduce the use of plastics, especially grocery bags and water bottles, which are created by using enormous amounts of fossil fuels.

People can take action within their communities by writing to public officials or serving on public boards and councils to

- encourage energy efficiency and the use of alternative energy sources in public buildings
- request amenities for bicyclists such as the installation of bike racks in public areas and the construction of bike lanes

- promote carpooling lanes and plans
- encourage utility companies to promote energy efficiency and alternative energy sources.

U.S. citizens can also encourage action by:

- monitoring and responding to their newspapers' coverage of global warming by:
  - stressing the need for the United States to become a leader in reducing greenhouse gas emissions
  - outlining the facts in response to stories that diminish the seriousness of climate change;
- contacting government leaders by e-mail, fax, or telephone, including
  - federal politicians—the president, senators, and congressional representatives—to encourage them to take action on reducing greenhouse gas emissions
  - state politicians—the governor, state legislators, and public utility regulators—to promote energy efficiency, the development of alternative energy sources, and mass transportation
  - all government leaders, to push them to encourage industry to reduce greenhouse gas emissions.

WRAP-UP

Climate scientists agree that global warming is happening and that it is largely caused by human activities. Because human activities are promoting warming, changing those activities can reduce it. The first step is for society to become more energy efficient by improving existing technologies and developing new ones. The next step is to develop and improve non carbon based technologies such as solar, wind, and eventually fuel cells and many other innovations. Carbon sequestration technologies that remove human-created carbon gases from the atmosphere can be improved. With so much evidence of warming emerging, particularly in the Arctic, the United States and all the nations of the world will need to decide on a strategy and provide the resources needed to make it work.

PART THREE

CHEMICAL POLLUTION
OF THE ARCTIC

Arctic Chemical Pollution

Although the polar regions are remote, they are not isolated from the wastes of modern society, as will be seen in this chapter. The Antarctic has little pollution because so little of its land has been developed. But the Arctic receives its air and water from the world's most industrialized nations, resulting in a surprising amount of pollution.

SOURCES OF ARCTIC POLLUTION

Due to its distance from the developed lands, the Antarctic shows few traces of the pollution that plagues the rest of the world. The Antarctic is more protected from the populated areas by the Southern Ocean and Antarctic Circumpolar Current, which circles the continent rather than flows toward it, thereby keeping much of the world's pollution at bay.

This is not the case for the Arctic. Some Arctic pollutants come from the use of chemicals and metals by local industrial and mining activities and human settlements. But most pollution comes from the developed regions of the Northern Hemisphere. Air currents that circulate from the industrialized nations of Eurasia and North America into the north polar region bring with them the pollutants that form Arctic haze (as discussed in Chapter 6). Contaminants flow into the Arctic via large rivers, particularly in Russia, which are heavily developed with industries, urban centers, and intensive agriculture. Man-made chemicals are frozen into ice at the river's mouth or near coastal regions and are carried around the Arctic Ocean basin by currents. Migratory birds and mammals transport the chemicals they obtain farther south in the winter when they fly to the Arctic in the summer. Pollution that mars a region or nation far from where the pollution originated is called **transboundary pollution**, which refers to the movement of contaminants across political borders, whether by air, rivers, or ocean currents.

Once they arrive in the Arctic, the pollutants remain for a long time. Many of them are trapped in the dense, cold air that stagnates over the north during the winter months. The contaminants break down more slowly than they do in warmer climates, and so they can become highly concentrated. Because the Arctic Ocean does not take in or send out much water, the contaminants do not become diluted, nor are they carried away to the south. They may become frozen into sea ice or adhere to clays and sink to the bottom of the ocean, where they can remain indefinitely. Pollutants in the Arctic accumulate in animal tissues and may be passed up the food chain or may enter the environment when the animal dies and its flesh decomposes.

TOXIC ORGANIC CHEMICALS

Toxic organic chemicals are **biodegradable**: They can be broken down over time by bacteria into stable, nontoxic inorganic compounds, such as carbon dioxide (CO_2), water (H_2O), and ammonia. An estimated 30,000 to 70,000 such chemicals are produced globally, with Europe producing about 35% of the global total, more than any other region of the world. This covers a wide variety of compounds, including oil and gasoline and organic chemicals. Although biodegradable materials break down, the process may take a very long time.

Organisms often store the pollutants they ingest in their bodies. So much seawater passes through a mussel's system as it feeds, for example, that the chemicals become concentrated in the mussel's tissues at levels 100 to 10,000 times greater than their concentrations in seawater. An animal that eats mussels or other prey takes into its body all of the pollutants from each of the hundreds or thousands of animals that it eats in its lifetime, so that the chemicals become extremely concentrated in the animal's body. This process is called **bioaccumulation**. Animals at the highest trophic levels, including top carnivores such as large predatory fish, seals, and whales, may amass concentrations as great as one million times their seawater concentration. One compound was found to be 71 times more concentrated in polar bears than in the seals that make up their normal diet.

When it comes to safety, chemicals are treated differently depending on when they were first manufactured. Those first produced after 1981 must undergo safety testing, but existing chemicals produced before that time do not. For that reason, more than 90% of the chemicals in use have not been evaluated for basic safety. The effects of many compounds are not known, nor is there much information on how organisms react to two or more chemicals together. Some of these chemicals may lead to physiological disorders in humans and other mammals that cause reproductive problems, including infertility or spontaneous abortion (miscarriage), neurological disorders, immune system problems, developmental abnormalities, and many others. Chemicals that are a current or potential problem in the Arctic are described below.

Oil, Oil Spills, and Gasoline Additives

Oil and gas are naturally occurring substances in the environment, usually found in underground reservoirs. But they can become pollutants in the areas from which they are extracted or when they are being transported or used.

Oil spills, although uncommon, get a great deal of attention because of the enormous amount of damage they can cause. Oil spilled in the ocean spreads rapidly over the sea surface. The effect on marine organisms depends on the amount and type of oil, the weather and sea conditions, and the ecosystems where the spill takes place. Refined oil is more damaging and has longer-lasting effects than crude oil because compounds contained in the refined product or its breakdown products are toxic to organisms. In addition, components added to the oil during refining make the mixture even more deadly. One group of these components, **polynuclear aromatic hydrocarbons (PAHs)**, which are found in weathered crude or refined oil, can reduce spawning success in some fish. They are also linked to genetic damage, malformations, and reduced growth and mobility in other species.

Damage from an oil spill evolves with time. For the first day or two after a spill, the hydrocarbons evaporate off the oil and kill some nearby aquatic organisms, particularly larvae and young. For the next days and weeks, the oil that floats on the surface reduces the sunlight available for photosynthesis, which leads to a decrease in primary productivity. Oil-sensitive red and green algae are often killed. Floating globs of oil coat seabird feathers and mammal fur, possibly causing the animals to lose their buoyancy and insulation. Many of them drown or die of exposure. When oil-soaked birds preen their feathers, they ingest toxic compounds. Globs of oil clog fish gills and kill larvae. Some of the oil sinks and smothers bottom-dwelling organisms.

Where waves and currents are strong, they can break up spilled oil. However, oil that penetrates down into sandy beaches, or between rocks, may remain there indefinitely. Populations of organisms can recover over time. Plants and invertebrates that produce enormous numbers of young often recover quickly because there are lots of opportunities for the young to find a suitable place to live. Individual birds and mammals are lost to the spill, but others migrate into the area once it is clean, and typically the population recovers within a few years. However, some ecosystems or organisms may take several decades to recover.

Marine oil spills causes losses to people as well as ecosystems. Oil-damaged commercial fishing boats and fishing gear cost fishers money and strongly affect the size and quality of their catches. Fisheries recover fairly quickly from spills due to the high reproductive rates of most fish, but the taste of the fish is tainted by the flavor of oil.

The Exxon Valdez *Oil Spill*

Although it happened south of the Arctic, the *Exxon Valdez* oil spill of 1989, the largest in United States waters, is a good example of what can happen with a large oil spill in a cold marine environment. The *Exxon Valdez*, a large oil tanker, struck submerged rocks in a narrow, iceberg-filled passage in Prince William Sound near Valdez, Alaska. Within six hours of the collision, the tanker lost about 10.9 million gallons (40 million l) of oil, or 22% of her load. Due to the lack of nearby knowledgeable people and equipment, little remediation took place in the first three days. Most of the damage was done during that time as the oil spread freely. Natural cleansing processes were not effective because the oil was released into calm, protected water instead of the open ocean. Eventually, a crew of more than 10,000 people using containment booms, skimmer ships, bottom scrapers, and absorbent sheets arrived, but they were able to contain only 17% of the lost oil, which coated more than 1,100 miles (1,700 km) of shoreline. Some estuaries had oil 3.3 feet (1 m) deep in places. In all, the spill killed an estimated 250,000 seabirds, 900 bald eagles, 2,800 sea otters, 300 harbor seals, 23 whales, and untold numbers of fish. The spill wrecked the Sound's $150 million per year salmon, herring, and shrimp industry.

Prince William Sound is gradually returning to normal. Commercial fisheries are doing well, and wildlife is abundant. Or so it seems. Substantial subsurface oil lies beneath cobble beaches: It appears not to have degraded and is still toxic. Because water cannot penetrate the oil, nothing can live in the ground below it. Some local animal populations seem not to have recovered, including common loons, harbor seals, harbor ducks, and Pacific herring. Sea otters still get oil on their fur while digging up clams. Their bodies also contain elevated levels of petroleum byproducts.

The *Exxon Valdez* disaster brought about new regulations in the hope of avoiding a similar occurrence in the future. In the United States, the 1990 Oil Pollution Act was passed to increase safety standards and assist with emergency response planning in the hope of avoiding another similar disaster. New tankers are being built with double hulls so that if the outer layer of the ship is punctured, another layer of steel provides protection. In some regions, such as the town of Valdez, Alaska, tugboats escort ships until they reach open water. Vulnerable regions have more detailed emergency plans. Internationally, single-hulled tankers are being phased out by 2015. Some nations prohibit single-hulled ships from carrying the most damaging grades of oil.

The Trans-Alaska Pipeline

Oil spills also cause damage on dry land. The Trans-Alaska pipeline, which was designed to last 25 years but is now topping 30, pumps oil from Alaska's Prudhoe Bay oil field south to the Port of Valdez, a distance of 800 miles (1,300 km). The pipeline has about 500 leaks a year, most of which are minor and quickly detected and fixed. In March 2006, though, an aging portion of the pipeline corroded from the inside, creating a hole about the size of an almond. This segment of the pipeline had not been checked for corrosion since 1992. For at least five days, oil leaked unnoticed beneath the snow, while the warning alarm failed to sound. By the time a worker smelled oil and investigated, nearly two acres (8,100 sq. m) of tundra was coated by a slick created by as much as 267,000 gallons (1 million l) of crude oil. Sixty crew members spent two weeks containing the spill, vacuuming up oil, and even trucking in fresh snow to absorb the remnants. Smaller leaks continue to happen frequently along the aging pipeline and must be cleaned up, as seen in the photo on page 117.

Cleanup of an August 2006 leak from an oil transit pipeline at the Prudhoe Bay oil field in the tundra involved workers using propane torches to burn off the oil. Small leaks like this one are common along the aging pipeline. *(AP Photo / Al Grillo)*

Oil Leaks and Small Spills

Certainly a major oil spill is a disaster, but about 10 times more oil enters the oceans from chronic, smaller-scale leaks than from major spills. This includes discharge from normal ship operations, such as flushing ballast water; spillage and waste from oil drilling and production platforms; leaks from the outboard motors of small boats; jettisoned aircraft fuel; and pollutants that are rained out of the atmosphere. By far, the largest source of oil in the oceans is the day-to-day runoff from roadways and other land surfaces. About 16 million gallons (61 million l) of oil are carried by rivers and streams into North American coastal waters each year. Oil and other pollutants also enter the oceans when they are dumped illegally.

The effects of these small additions of oil are less well known than the effects of major spills. The stresses caused by exposure to oil make animals more vulnerable to other problems that kill them later on. For example, low-level exposure to oil has been found to reduce the survival and reproductive success of seabirds and some marine mammals. Estimates are that hundreds of thousands of birds are killed by small oil slicks each year.

Persistent Organic Pollutants (POPs)

Persistent organic pollutants (POPs) are man-made compounds contained in pesticides, flame retardants, industrial solvents, and cleaning fluids. POPs are called persistent because they do not biodegrade or dissipate in the environment. The approach for the chemical industry and society at large has been to think that the chemicals are "safe until proven otherwise," even though many chemicals that were previously on the market have proven not to be safe.

POPs travel easily and are spread all around the Earth. In warm regions, the chemicals evaporate and enter the atmosphere. Once in the air, POPs may travel anywhere, even thousands of miles (km) from where they were first generated. The compounds eventually rain out of the atmosphere or attach to dust particles and are blown into lakes and streams. POPs may accumulate in bottom sediments. As a result, POPs are found in high levels even in animals and people that inhabit remote areas far from where the compounds originated. Researchers in the 1980s were shocked to discover that the breast milk of Canadian Inuits, which they analyzed because they needed a control and assumed quantities of POPs would be minimal, had high concentrations of these toxins. Because of their position high in the food web, polar bears carry high concentrations of toxic chemicals.

POPs are extremely effective at bioaccumulation: They reach higher concentrations at each trophic level as they move up the food chain. The compounds accumulate more readily in marine environments because they are easily absorbed by plankton. Concentrations are especially high in top predators that consume aquatic organisms such as whales, seals, and dolphins and fish-eating birds such as eagles, hawks, and gulls. Animals with long life spans, such as whales, build up the chemicals over a long period of time.

Most POPs do not dissolve in water, but they are soluble in fats and so are stored in body fat. Because Arctic animals build up fat when food is available and then use it for energy when they are molting, breeding, and hibernating, POPs are most likely to become a problem during lean times, when animals metabolize their fat reserves. When the fat breaks down, the chemicals enter the bloodstream and can damage the brain, liver, and other organs. In mammals, POPs are passed from mother to offspring during pregnancy and nursing. Even low-level exposures can be harmful to fetuses and during neonatal periods when mammals feed on chemical-laden mother's milk.

Some of the best known POPs have already been banned due to the environmental damage they cause. **Dichlorodiphenyltrichloroethane (DDT)** was a commonly used pesticide after World

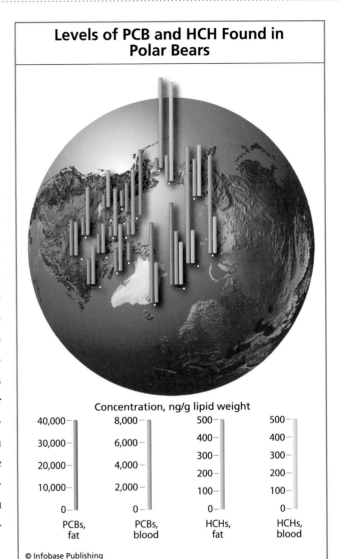

Levels of polychlorinated biphenyls (PCB) and hexachlorohexane (HCH) in adult female polar bears around the Arctic. Concentrations of PCBs in bears in the Svalbard archipelago were five times higher in fat than in blood from the same animal.

War II. It was extremely effective at controlling typhus, malaria, and other insect-borne diseases and was liberally sprayed on plants and ponds to kill unwanted insects. DDT bioaccumulates very effectively. Although the chemical was extremely dilute in waterways (about 0.00005 ppm), it concentrated in algae and aquatic plants to levels of about 0.04 ppm. Small fish that grazed on the algae and plants concentrated the pesticide to about 0.2 to 1.2 ppm, and top carnivores amassed DDT concentrations of 3 to 76 ppm.

Female birds were especially susceptible to the toxin because it interfered with their egg-laying ability. Peregrine falcons, bald eagles, barn owls, and kingfishers are just a few of the birds that laid eggs with shells so thin, they would break when the mother bird sat on them. The populations of these birds plummeted, and many of them were placed on the **endangered species** list. (An endangered species is one that is threatened with extinction.) Public outcry led DDT to be banned in the United States in 1973. Since then, the populations of affected birds have been recovering. DDT has now been banned in most countries but currently has very limited use in countries where malaria is rampant.

Polychlorinated biphenyls (PCBs) are extremely stable, water soluble compounds that were introduced in the 1920s. The chemicals were used primarily to insulate electrical equipment but were also used as flame retardants. When they were developed, PCBs were known to be toxic, but they were never intended to be released into the environment. Not surprisingly, however, the chemicals leaked from the equipment and from waste disposal sites.

Although PCBs have been banned in industrialized nations for decades, they are still everywhere in the environment. The chemicals' stability allows them to remain in soil and water bodies for many years, and their ability to bioaccumulate keeps them in the food web. Fortunately, concentrations of PCBs are dropping as the compounds become attached to sediments and are buried in lake bottoms.

As older chemicals with known toxic effects are being phased out, new POPs are continually coming on the market. The new chemicals include brominated flame retardants (BFRs); polybrominated diphenyl ether flame retardants (PBDEs); perfluorinated compounds (PFOs; used in TVs, computers, and cooking pans); polychlorinated naphthalenes (PCNs); and the pesticide endosulfan. Most of these chemicals are now measurable in the environment in small amounts and are accumulating. BFR levels will likely reach PCB levels in 10 to 20 years. Some of these new chemicals are also found to be harmful. The health effects of toxic chemicals are described in Chapter 11.

Since May 2004, POPs have been regulated under the Stockholm Convention on Persistent Organic Pollutants. Ratifying nations have agreed to reduce or eliminate the production or release of the ones labeled as the "Dirty Dozen": aldrin, chlordane, DDT, dieldrin, endrin, heptachlor, hexachlorobenzene, mirex, toxaphene, PCBs, **dioxins**, and furans. (Dioxins are byproducts of the manufacture of other materials.) The participating nations are also working to identify other POPs that should be added to the list. New substances that are being considered for addition are the flame retardants penta-BDE and hexa-BB; the pesticide chlordecone; and hexachlorohexane (HCH), the active ingredient in the pesticide lindane, which is used for treatment of head lice. By the terms of the convention, DDT will continue to be used, but only in tiny quantities to prevent the spread of malaria. The Stockholm Convention has been ratified by the European Community, the United Kingdom, and many developing nations.

The United States has not ratified the treaty, although most of the chemicals listed so far are already banned. Other chemicals have been banned as well. Since 2004, no PBDEs have been produced in the United States, but the nation still uses the chemical from its stockpiles. Europe has banned two forms of PBDEs.

HEAVY METALS

Most heavy metals are naturally present in low concentrations in the environment. Iron and aluminum, for example, are important components of many types of rock; and mercury and lead are spewed out by volcanoes. Plants and animals require tiny amounts of some heavy metals to carry out their life processes. Hemoglobin, the molecule that transports oxygen in the blood, utilizes iron. Many enzymes contain zinc. Other heavy metals required for life processes include copper, vanadium, and cobalt. Mercury, lead, and cadmium are not used by plants or animals and are toxic even in minute amounts. Even biologically useful heavy metals are toxic in high enough quantities. Because they bioaccumulate, heavy metals are especially dangerous to animals that feed high on the food chain.

Human activities discharge heavy metals into the environment. Burning coal, fuel oils, fuel additives, and trash releases heavy metals into the air, as does manufacturing steel and iron. These metals eventually fall or are rained out of the atmosphere. Runoff from the land brings heavy metals from atmospheric fallout, mines and metal refineries, urban areas, human waste, landfills, and contaminated sediments into rivers that then carry the heavy metals into the seas.

Mercury is probably the most damaging heavy metal. The most hazardous form is mercury that is released into the atmosphere by the combustion of coal and in municipal and medical wastes. Once airborne, the metal cools and turns into aerosol droplets that may travel hundreds of miles. Eventually, the droplets fall to the ground or into the water and wind up in sediment. Bacteria then convert this mercury into organic mercury, usually the dangerous **methyl mercury**.

Methyl mercury is extremely toxic. It is poisonous to some algae and to the larvae of some small invertebrates. The compound is easily absorbed through the skin, lungs, and intestines of animals. Methyl mercury bioaccumulates in the top predators that people eat, such as tuna. In humans, methyl mercury causes brain, liver, and kidney damage. Recognition of the dangers of mercury to human health resulted in a great decrease in global mercury production beginning in 1990. Unfortunately, mercury pollution is increasing in the Arctic, especially in marine birds and mammals in the Canadian Arctic and western Greenland, probably due to increased emissions from coal-fired power plants in Asia.

Lead is the most common toxic material found in humans, and enormous amounts are produced each year. Lead, as tetraethyl lead, was used as a gasoline additive worldwide until its danger to human health was recognized. Leaded gasoline has been banned in many countries since the late 1970s, but it is still in use in Russia and some other nations. Lead has also been phased out of use in paints. Still, the metal is ubiquitous in computer screens, electronics, batteries, medical equipment, and myriad other modern technologies from which it can easily seep into the environment. Lead enters the Arctic from atmospheric fallout or from industrial waste, landfills, and gasoline residue. Lead shot used for hunting is a continuing source of lead contamination in the Arctic and may be the primary source of lead in the diet of the people of Greenland. The metal is not toxic to lower organisms and does not seem to bioaccumulate. Lead causes nervous system, brain, and blood disorders in humans, especially in children.

Tributyltin (TBT) is a stabilizer in plastics and a major ingredient in the antifouling paint that is used on the hulls of ocean-going ships to keep barnacles and other organisms from growing on them. (These ships may also enter freshwater rivers and lakes.) Used in this way, the compound is extremely toxic to aquatic life. Concentrations of other metals such as platinum, palladium, and rhodium have increased in Greenland since the 1970s. High levels of cadmium are found in some Arctic seabirds.

WRAP-UP

Most people imagine that the polar regions are pristine, far removed from the pollutants of modern society. Although these regions are cleaner than many locations on Earth, local activities in polar regions emit pollutants; and, more importantly, atmospheric circulation, rivers, and ocean currents circulate pollutants into the regions, particularly the Arctic. Both the Arctic animals and Inuit people who are at the top of the food chain have very high concentrations of many toxic chemicals. Some of the most toxic chemicals have been banned; but others are relatively new to the market, and their effects are not yet known. The accumulation of these pollutants has a large effect on the wildlife and people of the Far North, which will be the topic of the following chapter.

The Effects of Chemicals on Arctic Wildlife

Contamination of the Arctic has become an increasingly serious issue, as will be seen in this chapter. The harsh living conditions and unique adaptations of Arctic plants and animals have made them especially vulnerable to environmental contamination. Many Arctic animals are exposed to an increasingly wide range of pollutants. Chemicals, heavy metals, and even radioactive materials are accumulating in animal tissues, soils, and water. Top predators, including some whales, polar bears, birds of prey, and some fish species, are known to contain contaminant levels that exceed international thresholds.

FACTORS THAT INCREASE HEALTH RISKS

The vulnerability of animals to the health effects of chemical pollutants varies by diet, trophic level, and stage of life. Regarding diet, animals that eat fish and marine mammals have high levels of organic chemicals and mercury. For example, those species that eat invertebrates have high amounts of cadmium, a heavy metal associated with bone and renal disease.

Arctic mammals that live at high trophic levels, such as some seals, polar bears, and predatory fish, bioaccumulate large amounts of toxic materials. The chemicals are stored in their fat and enter the animals' systems whenever the fat is metabolized. Because Arctic animals survive in the harsh climate in part because they store fat when food is available and metabolize the fat for energy when they need it, they are likely to receive a large pulse of chemicals at various times in their lives—for example, when food is scarce during the winter.

Chemicals also enter the animals' systems during certain stages of their life cycles. Because in many large mammals the length of time between birth and sexual maturity is relatively long—often three to four years, with long periods of time between births—females have time to accumulate a large amount of chemicals in their body fat. When the females utilize the fat during pregnancy or nursing, they pass these chemicals on to their young. Young mammals in the uterus and those that are nursing are most susceptible to damage from chemicals because their cells are rapidly growing, and their organs and brains are developing. In birds, the greatest damage occurs before the chick hatches. Sometimes the effects of chemicals are seen in the young, but sometimes the effects do not appear until the organism has reached adulthood. If harm comes to a female ovary, for example, damage to the egg (and consequently the young) may not appear until years later, when the animal reproduces.

HEALTH EFFECTS OF CHEMICAL POLLUTANTS

Toxic chemicals can have many different types of effects on animals. Some of these materials are **carcinogens**, the chemical or physical substances that cause **cancer** (the condition in which cells grow uncontrollably). Carcinogens can be chemical, including chemical emissions from industry, pollutants from cars and homes, and tobacco smoke. Carcinogens can also be physical substances, such as the UV radiation from sunlight, X-rays, and the radiation from radioactive materials found in the Earth. People and animals are also more likely to get cancer if they have a genetic predisposition to the disease: That is, they carry one or more genes that make them more vulnerable than the general population. People and animals are also more vulnerable to cancer if their overall health is not good. Adult cancers are ordinarily the result of years of collective damage to cells. Cancers in young animals or people are thought to be the result of exposure to toxins during the periods of growth, such as during fetal or neonatal development or childhood. Chemicals such as benzene, the gasoline additive methyl tertiary butyl ether (MTBE), and several persistent organic pollutants (POPs) are classified by the Environmental Protection Agency (EPA) as known or likely carcinogens.

Another important health risk from chemical pollutants is the interruption of the **endocrine system,** or endocrine disruption. This system regulates many of the body's functions, including growth, development, and maturation, by sending out **hormones** as chemical messengers. Hormones are released into the blood stream in carefully measured amounts by the endocrine glands, which include the pituitary, thyroid, and adrenal glands, the thymus, the pancreas, the ovaries, and the testes. Each type of hormone travels until it reaches a cell with a receptor that it fits, like a key in a lock. This allows the hormone to "turn on" the cell and stimulate it to produce a certain protein or to multiply.

Hormones are especially important in the growth of young organisms. In mammals, birds, reptiles, and amphibians, the development of a fertilized egg into a healthy young organism depends on minute amounts of hormones performing the right task at the right time. Receiving the right amount of hormone from the testes or ovaries at the right developmental stage is how boys develop into men and girls into women. Only miniscule amounts of a hormone are necessary for that hormone to do its work, often parts per billion (ppb) or even parts per trillion (ppt). Too much or too little thyroid hormone at a certain time will permanently damage the brain of a developing mammal. Hormone disruption can also damage immune systems.

The key-in-the-lock analogy that is used to describe how hormones and their receptors work is not entirely accurate because the lock (the receptor) is fairly open and may accept more than one key. In the human body, there is ordinarily only one "key" hormone for each receptor type. But some receptors respond to chemicals manufactured outside the body. Chemicals manufactured outside the body that mimic hormones and interfere with the normal functions of the endocrine system are called **endocrine disruptors**. Because hormones are effective in such tiny quantities, endocrine disruptors need only be present in miniscule quantities to cause damage to living creatures. An endocrine disruptor might block a hormone from doing its job in a receptor. It might, for example, give a signal that is too strong and cause the cell to do something it should not do or do what it should do at the wrong time. It also might give a signal that is too weak and also comes at the wrong time.

Any part of the endocrine system can be affected by endocrine disruptors. Hormones control neurological function, the immune system, internal organs, hunger and thirst, metabolism, growth, fertility, gender, sex drive, pregnancy, day and night cycles, behavior, and the ability to react to environmental conditions. The reproductive hormones regulate the gender of offspring and the development of sex organs. **Estrogens**, the female sex hormones in vertebrates, trigger the development of the sex organs and control the reproductive cycle. The estrogen receptor allows so many chemicals to bind to it that it has been called "promiscuous." **Androgens**, which are male sex hormones, develop and regulate the functioning of the male sex organs. Thyroid hormones play a role in regulating metabolism, growth, neural/brain development, and reproduction. In cetaceans, these hormones regulate heat loss, molting, and hair growth. The sex hormones also affect bone health.

The substitution of an artificial chemical for a sex hormone can have many negative effects on an animal. The effects on the reproductive system include diminished fertility, reduced sperm production, altered hormone levels, decline in offspring numbers and survival, increases in deformities (particularly of the reproductive system), offspring deaths, and even **hermaphroditism**—a condition where an animal has both male and female sex organs. After the parents' exposure to environmental estrogens, the numbers of males and females born may be skewed, with many more males than females or more females than males being born. The substitution of an artificial chemical for a thyroid hormone or neurotransmitter results in changes in movement, feeding, predator avoidance, learning and memory, and social interactions.

Many POPs are endocrine disruptors, including polychlorinated biphenyls (PCBs) and dichlorodiphenyltrichloroethane (DDT). Experiments in laboratory animals such as mice indicate that polybrominated diphenyl ether flame retardants (PBDEs) attack the sex and thyroid glands and impact motor skills and brain function. Heavy metals can also be endocrine disruptors. Tributlytin (TBT) is not only toxic to marine life, it is an endocrine disruptor at low doses that causes severe reproductive effects in aquatic organisms. Exposed females of some species of snails (from the order Prosobranchia) may grow penises or experience other types of masculinization. A relatively large number of snails and dogwhelks with these effects have been reported in northern Norway, and TBT levels are high in the blue mussel (*Mytilus edulis*). Because the use of TBT in Iceland now has been restricted to large vessels, the number of masculinized mussels has declined in the region. In mammals, including humans, TBT brings about immune system decline. In higher doses, the compound causes neural, respiratory, and psychological disturbances, plus abdominal pain and vomiting, among other problems.

Toxic chemicals can also alter an organism's immune response so that it has less resistance to common bacterial and viral diseases. These chemicals can interfere with the ability of an organism to utilize Vitamin A, which is required by almost every tissue in the body for growth and development, normal vision, reproduction, cell differentiation, and immunity. Chemicals—such as PCBs and dioxin—and heavy metals—such as cadmium—plus mixtures of various toxins interfere with Vitamin A in the body.

EFFECTS ON ARCTIC ANIMALS AND PEOPLE

Due to difficulties inherent in studying Arctic animals, many more studies have been done on the effects of chemicals on organisms outside the Arctic. It is extremely likely that the effects of chemicals on other animals can be generalized to Arctic animals. To understand the effects of chemicals on health, scientists can study animals in laboratory experiments or in the wild.

Laboratory experiments often provide scientists with the best information on the health effects of specific chemicals on specific organisms, but these experiments are limited in what they show. Laboratory animals such as rats and mice react differently to chemicals than do wild animals. For example, marine mammals are thought to be much more sensitive to synthetic chemicals than rats because rats have evolved to live in the human environment. Most lab experiments study the effects of a large dose of a single chemical on a group of animals, whereas in the wild, organisms are more likely to experience low levels of a pollutant over a long period of time. Wild animals are exposed to chemicals in mixtures, which may magnify the health effects. Of great concern is the likelihood that the new chemicals designed to replace the POPs that have been banned may be especially dangerous when added to an environment that already has high concentrations of old chemicals.

Wild animals are not only exposed to toxic compounds but to other stressors as well. Some of these stressors are part of everyday life, like finding enough to eat or avoiding being eaten. But Arctic organisms experience greater environmental stress than many other organisms because they live in such difficult conditions. Long winters, hibernation, migration, and many other factors are significant stressors in their lives. Human activities that lead to global warming, habitat loss, and reduced food supply also increase stress on wild animals. Stressors combined with the effects of toxic chemicals may cause an organism to experience reduced reproductive success and increase the likelihood of disease, death, and population reductions.

Two types of scientific studies on chemical contaminants have been done directly on Arctic animals. In one type of study, scientists analyze levels of contaminants in the animals' bodies, although, for ethical or practical reasons, they most often restrict their studies to animals that are stranded or dead. As a result, contamination levels in these organisms may not be representative of the general population.

In the second type of study, researchers look at toxic chemical damage by using certain biomarkers, traits that are caused by the chemicals but that are relatively easy to study. Biomarkers in Arctic animals include immune system function, thyroid and stress hormone levels, and vitamin A concentrations. Bone mineral density is a measure of general bone health, which affects the ability of an organism to bear weight and may be damaged by endocrine disruptors.

The effects of toxic chemicals on different groups of Arctic organisms are described in the following sections.

Seals, Sea Lions, and Walruses

Pinnipeds are especially at risk from toxic chemicals because they live at a high trophic level, store body fat, reach sexual maturity relatively late, go a long time between births, and live long lives. While seal pups nurse, the mother fasts or eats little, so the milk she provides for her pups comes from her blubber and will be tainted by toxic chemicals if her fat contains them.

In pinnipeds, pollutants have been shown to damage many body parts, including the skeleton, adrenal glands, and reproductive and immune systems. Pollutants have also been associated with changes in vitamin A and thyroid hormone levels. Populations of some seal species are currently in decline, and toxic chemicals may be partly responsible. Numbers of Steller's sea lions are falling; and while the blame cannot unequivocally be placed on toxic chemicals, the animals' tissues are known to be contaminated with mercury, PCBs, DDT, chlordane, butylins, and hexachlorobenzene. PCBs have been shown to cause lower Vitamin A levels and immune and reproductive problems in harbor seals. While the presence of DDT and PCBs has been declining in the environment, levels of the newer chemicals created to replace them have not been analyzed: These substances may have negative effects no one yet knows about.

Scientists speculate that recent pinniped mass deaths are the result of contaminants that weaken the animals' immune systems and make them more susceptible to illness. The mass deaths of 17,000 North and Baltic harbor seals (*Phoca vitulina*) in northwestern Europe in the 1980s were caused by morbillivirus, a virus associated with distemper. Scientists think that virus may have been able to run rampant through the population because the animals' immune system response had been compromised by exposure to toxic chemicals.

Whales

Toothed whales are top predators and accumulate high concentrations of chemicals in their bodies. Among the toothed whales, more is known about beluga whales, seen in the photo on page 133, and chemical exposure because these animals live along shallow coasts and in river inlets and so are relatively easily accessible. These Arctic and subarctic whales live for 30 to 50 years in waters that are often heavily contaminated. Northern beluga whales tend to migrate, but the southernmost group stays all year round in the St. Lawrence estuary of Canada, which is one of the most heavily industrialized regions in the world and is part of the Great Lakes system. The estuary's beluga population is estimated to have once been 50,000, before being decimated by hunting. The whales were given endangered status, complete with protections, in 1983; but the population continued to decline. Numbering 5,000 in the 1970s, the current population is only 500 to 700. The culprit is likely the water in which the whales swim, which is full of known carcinogens and endocrine disruptors.

Besides fishing and hunting, beluga whales dig in sediments for the small invertebrates that they find there. Heavy metals and synthetic chemicals attach to sediments and are taken up by the small animals and then eaten by the whales. Estuary whales have a level of overall contamination of man-made chemicals that is many times higher than the more northerly populations. St. Lawrence estuary belugas are so contaminated with organochlorine pesticides, polynuclear aromatic hydrocarbons (PAHs), and heavy metals that when some of the whales die their corpses are treated as toxic waste. The levels of new chemicals in St. Lawrence belugas are considered low, but they are still 10 to 25 times higher than in northern whales. These levels are predicted to increase along with demand for the flame retardant products.

Cancer is normally rare in cetaceans, but St. Lawrence estuary beluga whales have a cancer rate similar to that of humans, domestic cats, and cattle. Betweem 1983 amd 1998, 27% of all dead beluga whales in the estuary were found to have cancer, although not all died

Beluga whales are distinctive for their white color. Because they live in coastal areas as far south as the St. Lawrence Estuary of Canada, they are among the best known of the toothed whales. *(Gvictoria / Dreamstime.com)*

of the disease. Among this group was the first case of breast cancer ever seen in a cetacean. St. Lawrence belugas show other effects of chemicals, including lesions on the hormone-producing glands, bacterial infections, parasites, and reproductive and immune problems. The only true hermaphroditic cetacean ever found was a beluga whale that had both two testicles and two ovaries.

Although they live in an area significantly south of the Arctic, St. Lawrence belugas may foreshadow the future for the Arctic belugas if pollution into the region continues unabated. Some Arctic beluga populations actually have a higher concentration of some particular chemicals than the St. Lawrence group. In some cases, the chemical levels in the Arctic belugas' blood are high enough to potentially compromise their immune systems and place the whales at a greater risk of infectious diseases. Other whales have levels of PCBs, organochlorines, and mercury that are higher than the Health Canada guidelines for fish consumption.

Not surprisingly, chemical levels in Arctic whales continue to rise. A 2006 study of belugas and narwhals in Svalbard, an archipelago about midway between Norway and the North Pole, showed the highest levels of PCB and PBDE, and some pesticides ever measured in marine mammals in that area. The highest PBDE levels ever detected in Arctic marine mammals were recently found in the long-finned pilot whales that swim off the Faroe Islands, a Norwegian territory located northwest of Scotland.

Polar Bears

Polar bears have all the features of a species that is likely to suffer from toxic chemicals in the environment. They are top predators, feeding primarily on the blubber of ringed, bearded, and harp seals, and they live off their stored body fat for part of the year. Female bears give birth to their young relatively late and nurse for long periods.

Polar bears around the Arctic are heavily contaminated with chemicals, and different populations are exposed to different chemicals depending on their

Concentrations of POPs in Polar Bear Mothers' Milk

Concentrations, ng/g lipid weight

© Infobase Publishing

Concentrations of POPs in polar bear mothers' milk. The dark bar shows the concentration of the chemical in the milk of springtime new mothers that had lost their cubs by the following fall, and the light bar shows the concentration of the chemical in the milk of mothers that still had their cubs the following fall.

location. Some populations have such high concentrations of PCBs that they are losing their ability to fight common infections. Svalbard polar bears, for example, have PCB concentrations as high as 80 ppm. Cubs whose mother's have high PCB levels in their milk are more likely to

The Effects of Chemicals Seen in Some Populations of Polar Bears

CHEMICAL	EFFECT
PCBs	Reduced size of sex organs in males and females
	Depressed immune system function
	Low thyroid hormone levels
	Changes in testosterone concentration in males
	Progesterone changes in females
	Osteoporosis
	Liver changes, including chronic inflammation
	Masculinization of sex organs
Organochlorine pesticides	Reduced size of sex organs in males and females
	Depressed immune system function
	Immune system changes
	Thyroid hormone alterations
	Vitamin A alterations
	Changes in testosterone concentration in males
	Decreased bone mineral density
	Altered cortisol (stress hormone) concentrations
	Increased follicles in spleen
PBDE	Hermaphroditism

die in their first year. High organochlorines also damage the bears' immune systems.

Newer chemicals such as the flame retardants PBDE and HBCD; other brominated flame retardants (BFRs); and fluorochemicals such as PFOs are also showing up in polar bears. Polar bears at Svalbard had 10 times the concentration of PBDE as Alaskan polar bears and four times more than Canadian polar bears. On Svalbard, three or four bears out of every 100 are hermaphroditic, with both male and female sex organs. The hermaphroditism has been linked directly with pollution and possibly with PBDE. No other studies have been done on the effects of other newer chemicals on Arctic polar bears.

Birds

Birds that eat at a high trophic level and that store the chemicals they consume in their fat are highly susceptible to damage from toxic chemicals. As with marine mammals, it is difficult to determine the effects of chemicals on birds, although in many cases the results seem similar. Because the chemicals are soluble in fat, contaminant levels can be studied in the egg yolks of unhatched seabird eggs. Scientists are finding high levels of many different chemicals in birds. As with mammals, young unborn birds are very susceptible to toxins as they develop.

Toxic chemicals in birds result in reduced calcium, which results in decreased bone density and more broken eggs. Altered thyroid hormones may decrease a bird's metabolic rate and increase its sensitivity to cold. Studies of quail show that males exposed to several different chemicals experienced changes in sexual behavior, reproduction, and immune function, and had altered neurotransmitters and steroid hormones. Female birds are very sensitive to female sex hormone mimics, which can reduce the thickness of eggshells, for example.

Gulls are common Arctic birds that have many traits that make them susceptible to chemicals. They are top predators with long life spans, low reproductive rates, and delayed onset of reproduction. Studies of gulls have linked high levels of organochlorines to decreased parental attentiveness, impaired courtship behavior, and neurological effects. The birds' DNA may also be affected.

When gulls in the Norwegian Arctic had high levels of PCBs and oxychlordane in their blood, the parents left the nest for longer periods for feeding trips. High oxychlordane reduced the number of gulls that returned to the same breeding ground. When oxychlordane in the environment was reduced by 60%, as it was between 1997 and 2000, many more gulls returned to breed.

Glaucous gulls (*Larus hyperboreus*) are top predators with a lifespan of 10 years. Glaucous gulls in Svalbard have alarmingly high PCB levels, which are correlated with immune suppression and adverse effects on reproduction, behavior, immune function, and development. Glaucous gulls that were fed contaminated eggs in experiments suffered damage to their DNA.

Glaucous gulls sometimes develop an asymmetry in their wings (wing symmetry is regulated by thyroid hormone). On Bear Island in the northeastern Atlantic, wing asymmetry is used as a good indicator of environmental quality. Since the late 1980s, many dead, dying, and abnormally behaving gulls have been found on the island. Breeding pairs have been reduced by half since 1997 on some parts of the cliff. Some other effects of chemicals in glaucous gulls on Bear Island include

- Female gulls with high organochlorine levels laid eggs earlier and were more likely to give birth to dead chicks.
- Adult gulls had lower survival rates as levels of chemicals such as DDE, PCB, HCB, and oxychlordane increased.
- Adult gulls with high organochlorides had reduced immune system function.
- Male gulls with high organochlorine levels had reduced thyroid hormones.
- Other effects included decreased feeding efficiency, decreased reproduction and survival, high nematode parasite load, and wing asymmetry.

Female great black-backed gulls (*Larus marinus*) from Norway who were found to have high levels of organochlorines laid eggs later in the season, suffered nest predation, and had a greater decline in egg volume than less contaminated females. It is likely that these findings mean lower overall reproductive success for the birds. A 2005 study of persistent chemicals in four gull species in northern Norway, including Svalbard and the Faroe Islands, prompted authorities to advise young women, pregnant and nursing women, and children not to eat the gulls' eggs and to advise others to limit consumption to an absolute minimum.

Indigenous Peoples

The diet of many Inuit people is dominated by their traditional foods—whales, seals, polar bears, and fatty fish. These creatures live at the top of a long marine food chain. The Inuit say that their blubbery diet has allowed them to survive for generations in the severe polar environment. As some Inuit have converted to a Western diet of processed food, they have, as have other native people, fallen victim to diabetes and heart and coronary disease—illnesses that were previously virtually unknown to them. However, although their native diet is clearly healthier for them, indigenous Arctic people are now being encouraged to greatly reduce the amount of traditional food they eat because of the contaminant load that has been found in their prey species. Arctic people and some animals living at a high trophic level have been found to have 200 toxic compounds in their bodies.

The Inuit have been found to have a concentration of PCBs and PCB metabolites at levels 70 times that of southern Canadians. Canadian public health researcher Eric Dewailly found that PCB and pesticide amounts in the breast milk of Arctic women were up to 10 times higher than in women from large Canadian cities. Dewailly also discovered that the bodies and breast milk of some people in Greenland met the technical definition of hazardous waste. Subtle effects are being observed in the nervous systems and behavior of infants that are thought to be caused by exposure to toxic chemicals in the womb. The United Nations Environmental Programme (UNEP) calls the Arctic people among the most exposed in the world.

Ingmar Egede, a well-traveled, multilingual Greenlander, tells Marla Cone in her 2005 book *Silent Snow: The Slow Poisoning of the Arctic*, "Anger is the overriding emotion among Arctic people who are aware of the pollution." He notes the irony that the countries that condemn the Arctic people for hunting whales are the same ones that are contaminating both the whales and the people.

WRAP-UP

Some Arctic organisms are more vulnerable to damage from toxic chemicals because of the way they live: They store fat to use at various times of the year or during their life cycle, eat high in the food web, reproduce relatively late, and have few young. People have been especially surprised at the levels of chemicals and their effects in some polar bears. While Arctic whales are feeling few effects relative to whales in industrialized areas such as the St. Lawrence estuary, the effects of toxic chemicals on St. Lawrence belugas are frightening and may be the beginning of a trend that will be seen in other, more remote, locations. Because toxic chemicals accumulate in the environment and in biological systems, the effects will only become more pronounced unless the release of the chemicals into the environment is curbed.

PART FOUR

OVERFISHING AND OVERHUNTING IN THE POLAR REGIONS

Threats to Fish and Fisheries

For most of human history, people hunted wild animals for protein and for materials for homes, clothing, and other necessities. While the explosion in human population in the past few centuries has required the substitution of farmed animals for wildlife as food, this has not yet happened with marine creatures. People still hunt wild fish from the seas and, while **aquaculture** (the raising and harvesting of seaweed, fish, and shellfish) is growing in importance, most seafood is still wild caught. This chapter explores overfishing in the Arctic and Antarctic regions.

OVERFISHING

A **fishery** is a particular species of fish from a particular region that can be commercially fished. An example is the Arctic cod fishery, which is distinct from the North Atlantic cod fishery because the fish are different species and live at different latitudes. How humans develop and exploit fisheries usually follows a familiar path. For centuries, local people have harvested their catch in nearby waters

Inuit fishing for salmon using their traditional spears, as shown in a photo taken between 1910 and 1925. *(Library of Congress)*

from the beach, by dropping a line through an ice hole, or by paddling a boat out a short distance from shore. All these techniques are used by subsistence fishers to feed their families and communities. Thanks to their reproductive strategy of producing large numbers of young, fish populations easily recover from this low-level harvesting.

In time, fishers from outside the region discover the fishery and bring more boats. So long as relatively few people are fishing, the catch per unit effort (weight of fish caught versus vessel days of fishing) is high. Fishing is easy, and the season is lucrative. However, once large-scale commercial interests discover a fishery, a traceable decline in the fish population follows. Initially, technologically advanced fishing boats and factory ships may increase the total catch, but in the long run too many fish are harvested, and the population decreases. Although the money and effort expended by the fishing fleet may increase, the catch per unit effort decreases.

Overfishing occurs when the catch per unit effort and the total catch both decline. Too often, the fish are harvested before they are old enough to reproduce or before they have spawned many times, and there are not enough breeding animals left to replenish the species. Ultimately, the fishery becomes commercially dead, meaning that it is no longer economically feasible to sustain large-scale fishing efforts. Regulations may be put in place in an attempt to allow the fishery to recover; but, by this time, it is usually too late.

A fishery is part of a larger ecosystem, so its decline is felt by the other organisms that depend on it. Because of the smaller numbers of fish to eat, birds and marine mammals may die of starvation. The loss of one species may also cause a drop in the population of other organisms. The decline in the Alaskan pollock (*Theragra chalcogramma*) population from an estimated 12.2 million tons (11 million metric tons) in 1988 to 6.5 million tons (5.9 million metric tons) in the early 2000s may be partially responsible for the Steller's sea lion's population drop of as much as 94% in some regions. The decline is thought to be so great because the animals must expend a lot more energy to get their daily meal, and there is not enough food available to fuel the sea lions on their longer treks.

When a fishery collapses, commercial fishers usually move on to a new one. The new fishery may not have been previously exploited on a large scale because it is found in deeper water or is situated in a more remote location. The collapse of the North Atlantic cod fisheries has led to the development of fisheries in the Arctic and Antarctic regions that previously had been minimally fished and is now putting pressure on many other species, including the Arctic cod. As more desirable fish have become scarce, even fish that were never before considered valuable are now at risk. The Alaskan pollock, a tasteless bottom fish, is now processed and flavored to become artificial crab, shrimp, and scallops and so now suffers from overfishing. With so few unexploited fisheries remaining, this pattern cannot continue indefinitely.

OVERFISHING IN THE ARCTIC

The Arctic contains some of the world's richest fishing grounds. Indigenous people have long fished all along the Arctic coastline, and fish has always been an important part of their diet. But the same pattern that affects fisheries in temperate waters has also shaped Arctic fisheries. Use of advanced technologies has increased the Arctic fish catch so that many of those fisheries are now being overfished. Overfishing in the Arctic has decreased levels of all marine catches to where they are at their lowest ever. With the large fish gone, and smaller and less mature fish being constantly harvested, too few mature adults are left to reproduce. The loss of so many Arctic fish has had a grim effect on the region's birds, seals, and other marine mammals, many of which are dying of starvation. Some of them die even more quickly when they are caught in fish nets and drown.

Fishing in the Arctic is commercially desirable because of the large quantities of a smaller number of species of fish than are found in warmer waters. The presence of fewer species reduces the fishers' **bycatch** intake. Bycatch are the fish that the fishers do not want because the fishers are not licensed to catch them, they are priced too low in the marketplace, or they are too small to keep. Bycatch is expensive to fishers because it takes time to discard the fish, and fishing unmarketable animals causes wear and tear on equipment. Bycatch is also hard on the ecosystem because many of these organisms may die before they can grow up to replenish the stock, and small fish that are low in the food web may die without nourishing larger animals. The United Nations estimates that about 25% of all fish that are caught are bycatch. Birds and mammals can also become bycatch when they get caught in fishing gear and drown as a result.

Alaskan waters provide half of the annual harvest of fish and seafood in the United States. While these areas are now well managed, in the past, factory fishing fleets from Japan and the Soviet Union caused the collapse of several fisheries. When one species was fished out, the fleet would move to another. The loss of so many fish has been blamed for diminished wildlife populations in the Bering Sea and elsewhere. Now the state has strict regulations, and most Alaskan fisheries are being fished responsibly. An annual quota is set for each species, and once the quota is reached, the fishers must stop fishing for that species. Thanks to these management practices, Alaskan salmon, which were once depleted, are now part of a well-managed, sustainable fishery.

Other Arctic seas are not so well controlled. In August 2004, the United Nations Environmental Programme (UNEP) issued a report on the environmental problems facing the Barents Sea. In the Barents, as in most other seas, overfishing is not the only problem. The problems, in order of importance, include

- ⊕ overfishing of cod and haddock despite regulations because patrolling the oceans is very difficult. However, this is much less of a problem than it was in the 1990s
- ⊕ high pollution levels, as high as in other European seas. These are likely to increase due to the expansion of the oil and gas industries in the area
- ⊕ radioactive waste storage, which could possibly contaminate the environment
- ⊕ the expansion of **alien** or **invasive species**, which can be introduced from the ballast waters of ships. Invasive species are introduced by human activities into a location where they are not native. The Red King Crab (*Paralithodes camtschaticus*), which was intentionally introduced into the Barents Sea, competes with both commercial and noncommercial species, and could bring about the loss of some fish stocks.

OVERFISHING IN THE SOUTHERN OCEAN

Fish in the waters around Antarctica swam in complete isolation from human predation until recently. There were no native people, and dangerous conditions in the Southern Ocean kept fishers from exploiting the region in great numbers. That situation has changed in recent decades, and now the waters of the Southern Ocean and Antarctic are a tremendous source of fish. While isolation allowed the fish to live in peace for millennia, this same isolation is now causing problems because it allows fishers to operate without much interference from the outside world.

Fisheries scientists in Argentina have called global attention to the depletion of the mackerel icefish (*Champsocephalus gunnari*) and to

Antarctic cod have special adaptations that keep them from freezing in the frigid Antarctic waters. These and some other Antarctic fish species are being overfished in some locations. *(Commander John Bortniak / NOAA Corps)*

violations of laws that were drafted to protect it. In a 2004 report in *La Nación*, these scientists reported that fishing fleets were operating out of control. Because mackerel icefish swim in large schools, they are easily netted. Sometimes seabirds such as petrel and albatross dive into a school of icefish that is surrounded by a net and are captured and drowned.

The fishery was first exploited in 1971. Its catch peaked in 1978 at 235,000 tons (212,000 metric tons). By 1991, the catch had fallen to 13,000 tons (11,700 metric tons). By 1992, the catch was only 66 tons (59 metric tons). Fishing of mackerel icefish off Antarctica is now strictly limited, although the fishery north of the Antarctic Circle, around the Heard and McDonald Islands, has been certified as being fished sustainably by Australian fisheries managers.

Besides overfishing, global warming presents a potential additional hardship for these unique animals. As discussed in Chapter 4, icefish are adapted to subfreezing waters. As the Antarctic's waters warm, the fish may not be able to adapt to the change. For both of these reasons, the future of Antarctic icefish is uncertain.

Argentina and other nations have warned of the decline of two species of toothfish for years. Marketed in the United States and elsewhere as the Chilean sea bass, this animal is actually two species of fish. The Antarctic toothfish (*Dissostichus mawsoni*) swims in the frigid waters around Antarctica and has "antifreeze proteins" to keep its blood from freezing. The more abundant Patagonian toothfish (*Dissostichus eleginoides*) swims in warmer waters farther north. Both of these species are heavily fished. They are among the species that replaced the North Atlantic cod on people's dinner tables after the collapse of that fishery.

Like other deepwater fish, these predators are slow to mature. They breed at 10 to 12 years and live until they are at least 45. A fully grown fish is large, just over 6.5 feet (2 m) long and 220 lbs. (100 kg). Long-lived, slowly maturing fish typically have low reproductive rates, and thus their populations are slow to recover from fishing pressure.

Toothfish are not easily netted and are mostly captured by longline fishing. A longline is a fishing line up to 50 miles (80 km) long, with many smaller lines projecting outward, each with thousands of hooks. The fish are taken off the line as they are reeled in. Longline fishing, with its miles of baited hooks, catches everything that swims or flies by. The baited hooks also attract seabirds, which swallow the hooks along with the food. The hook eventually kills them. As a result, populations of some seabirds, such as albatross and petrel, are now declining. Toothfish are also important to the diets of some large predators, such as whales and seals, so their decline is felt even higher up the food web.

Chilean sea bass is delicious and, it is a commercially desirable fish; but overfishing has now made these fish rare and difficult to catch. A single animal now brings up to $1,000, making it one of the most valuable fish in the sea. While there is a legal quota, the high prices have stimulated a lot of illegal fishing activity. In the mid to late 1990s, the illegal catch was two to three times that of the legal catch. The fishery is now better monitored by satellites, tighter import controls, and high-profile arrests. Nonetheless, pirate vessels continue to scour the southern seas, and a few stocks have already collapsed. Without better regulation, the entire fishery may collapse in a few years.

Overfishing is also a potential threat to an animal at a low trophic level—krill. Although humans do not eat krill, the fishing industry is finding other uses for these abundant creatures. Fish farmers who engage in aquaculture are increasingly using them to meet their enormous need for fish oil and fish meal. While fish farming is often good for taking pressure off wild fish stocks, every pound of farmed fish eats three pounds of wild small fish or zooplankton. The biotechnology industry is also interested in krill because they contain substances that may be beneficial for treating heart disease, premenstrual tension, and skin cancer. The fishing industry claims that krill are just beginning to be exploited and that there is no overfishing problem. Fisheries scientists say that krill are so important to the polar food webs that protective measures should be taken now before overfishing becomes a problem.

Krill populations have dropped by about 80% since the 1970s, according to a study by the British Antarctic Survey (BAS) published in *Nature* in 2004. Fishing can be blamed for very little of that population loss. The most likely cause is global warming, particularly the decline in sea ice along the Antarctic Peninsula, a key breeding ground for the krill. The long-term decline in Antarctic krill has resulted in an increase in salps in the Southern Ocean. While the salps have obviously benefited, these jellylike organisms are not a good source of food for fish. Organisms higher up the food web, such as seabirds and whales, have also declined. The less food there is available, the more susceptible to diseases animals become; and diseases that afflict marine organisms are on the rise.

WRAP-UP

Overfishing is rampant worldwide, although until recently, the polar regions have been mostly spared due to their remoteness and harsh conditions. The loss of fisheries in more temperate waters, such as the North Atlantic cod fishery, has caused fishers to harvest in waters that were once considered too remote and difficult to fish. Fish that were previously ignored, such as the mackerel icefish, are now endangered or commercially extinct. Fisheries can be managed, and after decades of being overfished, most Alaskan fisheries are doing well. In areas where overfishing occurs, such as the Bering Sea, repercussions are felt higher up the food web. For the oceans to remain healthy, well-managed fisheries are a necessity. Measures that should be taken include limiting the volume of the catch, restricting the age at which fish can be taken so they will have ample opportunity to reproduce and spawn many times, and minimizing bycatch.

Threats to Marine Mammals and Birds

Marine mammals were once taken from the sea in large numbers. Regulations governing which species can be hunted, and in what numbers, have allowed the populations of some of them to recover, but others are still threatened with extinction. In addition to the threats to polar marine birds, this chapter describes whaling and sealing and their impacts on marine mammal populations today. Although whaling and sealing have mostly been curtailed, obstacles to these mammals' recovery remain.

MARINE BIRDS

Populations of some marine birds in the polar regions are in decline due to a variety of factors. Most significant of these is the loss of birds as bycatch: This happens when hungry birds dive into a school of fish that has already been netted by fishing boats. The birds, unable to escape, then drown. Sometimes, they are hooked attempting to eat the bait on longlines. They may even become entangled in fragments of abandoned nets that float through the ocean. Invasive species, such as dogs or feral cats, may enter an area and eat bird eggs or young. These animals may bring bird populations into contact with new diseases against which they have no resistance.

The habitats of some birds suffer numerous disturbances: Warmer temperatures are destroying the ice floes that penguins travel on, for example. These birds sometimes have difficulty getting to the sea to feed due to increased numbers of icebergs blocking their path. Some polar habitats are becoming polluted by chemicals, which reduces reproductive success in many animals. Human development, among other changes to the environment, sometimes reduces or degrades habitat.

MARINE MAMMALS

Marine mammals have long been exploited by humans in the polar regions. Indigenous people hunted whales for thousands of years, eating their meat and using their oil for fuel and light, their bones for tools and construction, and their baleen as support for shelters. For centuries, Europeans hunted marine mammals, and marine mammal products were commonplace. Whales were hunted for their fur, oil, and meat. Seals and sea otters were trapped for their luxurious pelts, while walrus were taken for their ivory tusks.

Europeans hunted marine mammals intensely, resulting in enormous population declines. A few species were driven to, or close to, extinction. The numbers of marine mammals declined so precipitously that they were the only marine organisms that were given legal protection before the late twentieth century. Despite these protections, however, many marine mammal populations have not recovered: Globally, two-thirds of marine mammal species are classified as threatened. The reasons why some marine mammal species are unable to bounce back are varied and may include continued hunting, warming temperatures, invasive species, food shortages, and the spread of diseases from land into the marine environment.

Whaling

In the mid-nineteenth century, a time when commercial whaling was at its peak, whales were killed primarily for the oil they carried in their enormous heads. Whale oil burned bright, white, and clean in the lamps of the period. When oil was discovered below ground in Pennsylvania in 1859, the demand for whale oil plummeted in America and some other nations, but whaling continued in other countries for the oil and, later on, for the meat.

No one knows how many whales roamed the pre-nineteenth century oceans; but by 1900, it is estimated that there were 4.4 million large whales left. The introduction of factory ships before World War I expanded the number of whales that could be taken. Other ships could transport the whale products to shore, leaving the factory ships at sea, where they could continue to process whales incessantly. To match the increased speed of processing, faster hunting ships and more effective guns were developed. Whaling continued to be an important industry after World War II, when whale oil was an essential source of fat in Europe, and whale meat was a valuable part of the diet in Japan and Russia.

The demise of many of the larger whale species took place in the post–World War II era. The blue whale rapidly declined in the 1940s, the fin and humpback between 1955 and 1970, and the sei in later years. As the populations of the mammoth species declined, progressively smaller whales were the only ones remaining to be taken. The scarcity of large whales caused Europeans to end whaling in the early 1960s. Japan and the Soviet Union continued to whale as the last of the commercial whale fisheries were depleted. No factory ships sailed after 1978; by the 1980s, the international whale trade was dead, although small-scale coastal whaling continued. The National Marine Fisheries Service of the United States estimates that two million whales were killed by commercial whaling in the twentieth century.

All of the commercially valuable whales might be gone were it not for the public outcry. Warnings that the levels of harvest could not be maintained were sounded in the 1930s. The International Whaling Commission (IWC) was established in 1946 but did not successfully impose a moratorium on all commercial whaling until 1986. Today, 8 of the 11 species of commercially hunted whales are commercially extinct: Their numbers are so low, it is not in the interest of commercial whalers to hunt them.

Whales taken for scientific research are exempt from the whaling moratorium. Japan, where whale meat is a delicacy, takes hundreds of whales this way each year, mostly the small and relatively numerous minke whales, whose population the IWC estimates at around one million. Norway resumed whaling in 1993 and has since been increasing the quantity and diversity of the catch. According to Whalewatch, Japan, Norway, and Iceland killed over 1,400 whales in 2004, and that number is rising. These countries are now hunting humpback and fin whales and are increasing whaling in Antarctica. Japan killed 10 endangered fin whales in 2006 and planned to kill 60 in 2007. Also in 2007, the nation planned to begin killing 50 humpbacks each year for 18 years; again, they claim, for scientific research. Since the ban on whaling began, over 25,000 whales have been killed. Other countries are considering rejoining the hunt.

In addition to research whaling, the IWC allows subsistence whaling by aboriginal people, provided the population of the hunted whales is not too low. The IWC also sets aside whale sanctuaries, including the 8 million square miles (21 million sq. km) around Antarctica, a sanctuary that is not recognized by Japan. The IWC also funds whale research and promotes studies on methods that are used to kill whales; many of these methods are considered inhumane.

Despite the continuation of some whaling, the populations of a few species are rising. The greatest success story has been the eastern Pacific stock of the gray whale, which summers in the Arctic Ocean. It was removed from the endangered species list in 1993. The population is estimated to be about the same as at the beginning of the nineteenth century, between 17,000 and 23,000 animals, according to the National Oceanic and Atmospheric Administration (NOAA). This number is thought to be the stock's carrying capacity, meaning that its numbers ebb and flow with the food supply. Unfortunately, the western Pacific stock is still depleted, numbering only in the hundreds. The North Atlantic population was hunted to extinction 300 years ago.

Populations of some whales are still greatly reduced, even after decades of protection. The global population today of the largest animal that ever lived, the 100-foot-long blue whale, is below 5,000, under 1% of their original numbers. Some estimates put the number as low as 1,300. The pre-whaling Antarctic blue whale population is estimated to have been between 200,000 and 350,000; thousands were taken from the Antarctic during whaling times, mostly during the twentieth century. Blue whale recovery is likely hindered by PCBs that have been accumulating in the whales' bodies and that may cause premature death. In addition, the noise pollution created by ships and other ocean traffic makes communication between whales more

A whale, killed off the west coast of Iceland, lies over a fishing boat. The whaling ban, which protects most species, is being attacked by several whaling nations. *(AP Photo / Adam Butler)*

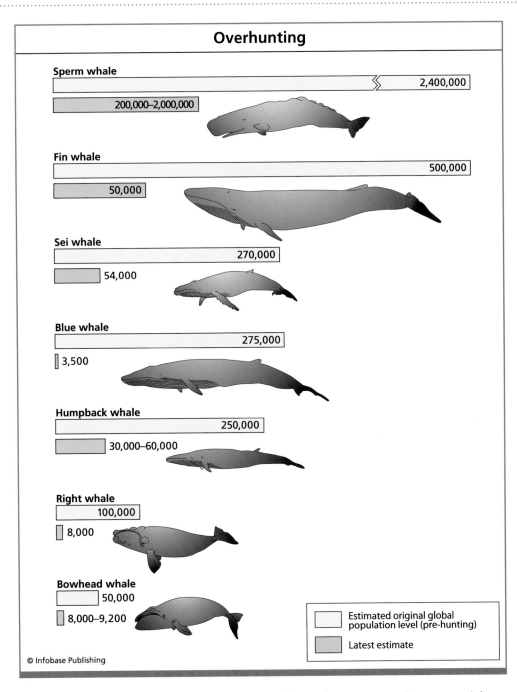

Overhunting

Sperm whale
2,400,000
200,000–2,000,000

Fin whale
500,000
50,000

Sei whale
270,000
54,000

Blue whale
275,000
3,500

Humpback whale
250,000
30,000–60,000

Right whale
100,000
8,000

Bowhead whale
50,000
8,000–9,200

Estimated original global population level (pre-hunting)

Latest estimate

© Infobase Publishing

Whales have been overhunted for centuries, and the 20th century saw the commercial extinction of several species. The numbers of species that are currently swimming in the sea are poorly known, and even less well known are the numbers that existed before commercial whaling. These numbers are estimates given by various groups.

Endangered, Threatened, and Vulnerable Polar Species

COMMON NAME	LOCATION	SCIENTIFIC NAME	LEVEL OF THREAT	CAUSE OF THREAT
Bowhead whale	Arctic	*Balaena mysticetus*	Endangered (some stocks)	Be, Pi, GW
Beluga whale	Arctic	*Delphinapterus leucas*	Vulnerable	H, Pw, Tb
Narwhal*	Arctic	*Monodon monoceros*	Data deficient	H
Sperm whale	Arctic	*Physeter macrocephalus*	Vulnerable	H, Be, Bn, I
Blue whale	Whole ocean	*Balaenoptera musculus*	Endangered	H, GW
Fin or finback whale	Whole ocean	*Balaenoptera physalus*	Endangered	H, Tc
Humpback whale	Whole ocean	*Megaptera novaeangliae*	Vulnerable	H, Be, Tc, Pn
Harbor porpoise	Arctic	*Phocoena phocoena*	Vulnerable	H, Be, Bn, Pw
Greenland shark	Arctic	*Somniosus microcephalus*	Near threatened	H, Bh, Bn, I
Polar bear	Arctic	*Ursus maritimus*	Vulnerable	HL/HD, H, Pc, Pi, I, Hd
Porbeagle	Arctic	*Lamna nasus*	Vulnerable	H, Bh, Bn, I
Macaroni penguin	Antarctic	*Eudyptes chrysolophus*	Vulnerable**	HL/HD, GW, Pw
Gentoo penguin	Antarctic	*Pygoscelis papua*	Near threatened	HL/HD, Bn, P, HD

Common name	Region	Scientific name	Status	Threat
Southern giant petrel	Antarctic	*Macronectes giganteus*	Vulnerable**	Bh, Pc, Hd
Sooty albatross	Antarctic	*Phoebetria palpebrata*	Endangered	Ip, D, Bh
White chinned petrel	Antarctic	*Procellaria aequinoctialis*	Vulnerable**	Ip, H, Bh, Bn
Indian yellow-nosed albatross	Antarctic	*Thalassarche carteri*	Endangered	Bh, D
Gray-headed albatross	Antarctic	*Thalassarche chrysostoma*	Vulnerable	Bh, GW
Black-browed albatross	Antarctic	*Thalassarche melanophris*	Endangered	Bh

Source: From the IUCN List, 2006

Key to Cause of Threat: H: harvesting; HL/HD: habitat loss, habitat degradation (could include loss of fisheries); Be: bycatch, entanglement; Bh: bycatch, hooking; Bn: bycatch, netting; D: introduced diseases; Hd: human disturbance (such as tourism); Ip: invasive species***, predators; P: pollution (general), Pc: pollution, chemical; Pi: pollution, industrial; Pn: pollution, noise; Pw: pollution, water; Tb: traffic disturbances, boat; Tc: traffic, vehicle collision; I: intrinsic factors such as slow growth, slow reproduction, limited reproductive success; GW: global warming

*The trend in the population of narwhals is not well known, but these animals are currently harvested.

**Listed by BirdLife International because population decreased by at least 30% over three generations.

***As an example, an introduced species such as house mice can threaten a bird population by attacking and killing the chicks.

difficult. Blue whales are examples of what happened to the gigantic baleen whales, but they are not isolated examples.

Fin whales have a current population of around 50,000 to 100,000 after an estimated 450,000 were taken in the twentieth century. It is estimated that there were once 400,000 in the Southern Hemisphere, and there are currently as many as 80,000 or as few as 2,000 today. The large discrepancy in estimates is because the whales live far from human activity and are very difficult to count. The current population of bowhead whales is estimated to range from about 8,000 to 9,200, down from around 50,000 before the advent of commercial whaling. During the twentieth century, more than 200,000 humpback whales were taken, reducing the global population by more than 90 percent: The IWC now estimates that there are between 5,900 and 16,800, but other estimates are as high as 60,000. There are an estimated 7,000 southern right whales remaining after tens of thousands were taken in the twentieth century. More than 215,000 sei whales were killed in the twentieth century. The current beluga population is around 100,000; their pre-whaling population estimate is unknown. No one knows how many sperm whales currently swim the seas, but estimates range from 200,000 to 2 million. These whales are doing relatively well because they are no longer hunted, they live in deeper water where there is less pollution, and they are not competing for prey with humans.

Japan and other pro-whaling nations are exerting constant pressure for the whaling ban to be lifted. They say that whale populations are recovering, so the ban is no longer needed. In June 2006, the nations of the International Whaling Commission voted not to resume whaling, but only because the pro-whaling nations did not have enough votes to overturn the ban. The resumption of more widespread whaling will continue to be a major issue in coming years.

Anti-whaling sentiment is still high in most countries. Some organizations want to continue the whaling ban based on the inherent cruelty of whaling. There is, they say, no way to hunt a large, semi-submerged, air-breathing animal humanely: Whales can take over an hour to die. Other organizations are opposed to whaling from an economic standpoint: Whale watching is a billion-dollar-a-year industry, involving nearly 10 million people in 87 countries, and this business could suffer economic damage if whaling were allowed to resume at previous levels.

Early in the last century, overexploitation of whales resulted in a rapid increase in krill predators such as fur seals. Following this shift in the predator balance, a return of the whales to pre-exploitation levels now presents a further problem arising from lower krill density.

The conservation status of some polar species, including whales, seals, and birds, is shown in the table on pages 158 and 159.

Sealing

Arctic seals are prey for a large number of animals, especially polar bears. There is archeological evidence of seal hunting by native Arctic residents as far back as 10,000 years ago. Seals have long been hunted for their thick, warm fur; for oil; for processing leather; and to make soap. Rich in protein, vitamin A, and iron, seal meat has been an important part of the Inuit diet.

Commercial sealing began in the sixteenth century and became an important economic activity by the late eighteenth century. By 1830, stocks of many seal species were already seriously depleted; by the beginning of the twentieth century, the populations of several species were reduced to dangerously low numbers. Initially, quotas were enacted in the United States and were somewhat effective, but protections became much stronger with the passage of the **1972 Marine Mammals Protection Act**. The act shielded all but the Alaskan northern fur seal from hunting, although by 1986 public pressure became so strong against sealing that even that industry collapsed. Indigenous hunters are allowed to take a small number of seals each year for food.

Arctic Seals

Public outrage nearly ended seal hunting in the 1980s (only 15,000 were killed in 1985), and the seal hunt is off in the United States and many other countries. But a few nations, notably Canada, Norway, and Greenland, continue to harvest seals; and since 1996, the quota has been increasing. In 2006, the quota allowed hunters to kill as many as 325,000 harp seals; 10,000 hooded seals; and 10,400 gray seals (*Halichoerus grypus*), a northern species that does not dwell on the ice; with an additional 10,000 permits for indigenous hunters. Even under these limits, sealers exceeded their quota by 1,000 animals. (Seal quotas are supposed to take into account that many more animals are killed illegally than the quotas allow.)

One reason the harp seal quota has been allowed to rise is that harp seals feed on Arctic cod, and an adult seal eats about one ton (900 kg) of sea creatures over its lifetime. Some fishers blame the inability of the cod population to recover from overfishing by humans on the growing population of harp seals; as a result, they recommend expanding the hunt. Conservationists respond that the cod population is low because they have been overfished, and the situation has little to do with the seals.

Some Canadian politicians, seal hunters, and fishers favor an increase in the seal quota to promote the economic well-being of the

Marine Mammal Protection Act, 1972

The precipitous decline of marine mammal populations, to the point of risking extinction, along with the negative publicity from photos of baby seals being clubbed to death, led the United States to search for a solution. In 1972, the United States established the Marine Mammals Protection Act. The act bans taking (defined as harvesting, hunting, capturing, or killing or attempting to kill) or importing any marine mammals or mammal product in United States territorial waters and fisheries. The act also makes it unlawful for any person or vessel subject to the jurisdiction of the United States to harvest any marine mammals on the high seas, except under a preexisting international treaty. There are two exceptions, both of them governed by strict guidelines: A few marine mammals may be caught for scientific research and public display, and a few may be caught by Alaskan natives for subsistence hunting and for creating and selling authentic native crafts and clothing. The act bans the importation of marine mammals and marine mammal products into the United States. Species or stocks must not be allowed to fall below their optimum sustainable population level; if they do, further measures, which might coastal communities that have already been hurt by the collapse of the cod fishery. People who had once made their livelihood in fishing can now change to sealing. A demand for seal coats has emerged as new markets for the fur have developed in Russia, Ukraine, Poland, and China.

Public pressure has brought about changes in the Canadian hunt since the 1970s. The youngest pups, those with white fur, are now off limits. Pups that are three weeks old, with black spotted silvery fur, are now the most in demand. Although the seals pups are still clubbed, they are no longer skinned alive. Some countries are working at the other end of the supply chain to ban selling products from the hunt. Americans and Europeans have prohibited the sale of products from seals for years.

Hunting is not the only activity that endangers seals. Commercial fishing and changing environmental conditions have reduced their food supply. The seals also become entangled in fishing gear, such as

include a total ban on hunting, must be taken to replenish the stock.

Marine mammals were not the only organisms that were suffering population declines. The **Endangered Species Act of 1973** requires that the government protect all animal and plant life threatened with extinction, including those that are likely to become endangered in the foreseeable future. The act also requires the conservation of the ecosystems that support threatened or endangered species. Marine species are administered by the National Marine Fisheries Service (NMFS). The Fish and Wildlife Service (FWS) administers terrestrial, freshwater, and migratory bird species. Species are listed after intense study and public comment. The act states that decisions on whether to include a species should be made on biological grounds, without concern for economic considerations. Once listed, the goal is for the species to recover so it can be removed from the list. Guidelines are provided for recovery. Federal agencies must consult with NMFS or FWS on any activity involving the species or their habitats. No one is allowed to take or harass any endangered species in the United States.

nets and lines. In addition, disease and pollution are eradicating them. Climate change endangers seal habitat by decreasing amount of ice or changing the water flow. Increasing oil and gas interests in these northern seas may degrade their environment, as may increased ship traffic in their habitats.

Antarctic Seals

Several species of Antarctic ice seals, including the Weddell and crabeater, were never widely hunted because their habitat is so remote from the rest of the world. But the Southern Ocean seals that live farther from Antarctica were not so fortunate. Elephant seals were hunted to near extinction in the nineteenth century, but the end of hunting has allowed the population to grow to around 600,000. Antarctic fur seals were hunted so heavily that they were thought to be extinct, but a small population of a few thousand was discovered on Bird Island. From these few, the population has recovered to an estimated two to four million animals and is thought to double every five years. Their recent population explosion may be related to the decline of baleen whale populations, which leaves more krill for the seals to eat. Some governments with interests in the Antarctic, including the United Kingdom, say that some of these protections should be lifted because the species is causing damage to vulnerable Antarctic plants.

Although populations of Antarctic ice seals are recovering, there are other problems facing them. Seals become entangled in fishing nets. Some Antarctic seals have relatively high levels of heavy metals in their bodies, although the concentrations are still much less than for seals in other oceans. Expansions of the Antarctic krill fishery could reduce the food available for the seals. Leopard seals, for example, are less competitive than other krill-eating seals and may suffer population declines. Global warming is a problem for Antarctic seals that live on pack ice as the amount of ice declines. Warmer temperatures are also likely to further reduce the krill populations, leaving less food for seals.

WRAP-UP

People nowadays are interested in and concerned about the condition of marine mammals such as cute baby seals, intelligent dolphins, and gigantic whales. Many species of these organisms have managed to survive by luck: the unknown population of the supposedly extinct Antarctic fur seals on Bird Island that led to the species' recovery, for example. Recognition of the problem, followed by the political action that people took during the twentieth century, played an even more important role in saving most whale species from extinction. After centuries of hunting, some species remain endangered and some are already extinct, but others are recovering. Some species, however, are not recovering, even though they are no longer hunted, due to a complex number of problems. These include warming temperatures, the loss of sea ice, pollution, and overfishing. Protecting marine mammal species from further losses means that people must understand and protect all aspects of the animals' environment.

PART FIVE

THE FUTURE OF
THE POLAR REGIONS

Protecting the Polar Regions

This chapter describes environmental protections that have been put in place for the Antarctic and Southern Ocean and those that are in place for the Arctic. Although both polar areas have been shielded from environmental problems due to their remoteness from the rest of the world, modern transportation and the amount of pollutants that are being released into the environment have reduced their isolation. Because Antarctica has never been owned by any single individual, company, or government, its jurisdiction is in many ways less complex than that of the Arctic, where several nations, each with its own special interests, come together like the segments of an orange.

PROTECTIONS GOVERNING ANTARCTICA AND THE SOUTHERN OCEAN

The Antarctic Treaty was first signed in 1959 by the 12 nations that were scientifically active in Antarctica during the International Geophysical Year of 1957 to 1958: Argentina, Australia, Belgium, Chile,

France, Japan, New Zealand, Norway, South Africa, the Soviet Union, the United Kingdom, and the United States. The treaty took effect in 1961 and has since been signed by 33 other nations.

The Antarctic Treaty governs the land and ice shelves in the area south of 60°S. The document sets aside Antarctica as a scientific preserve and prohibits military activity there. The treaty protects the

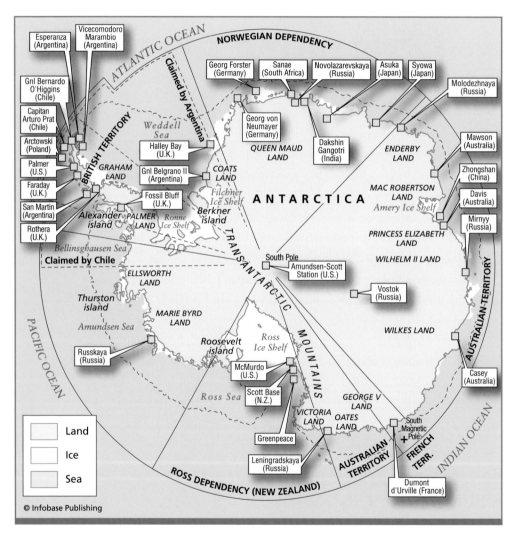

The scientific stations on Antarctica are the research bases for about 4,000 scientists.

life of the continent and the surrounding regions. Currently, about 4,000 scientists work at research stations on and around Antarctica. No nation is allowed to engage in secret activities on the continent and all areas must be open at all times to inspection.

The treaty and related agreements, known as the Antarctic Treaty System, include some 300 measures that have been adopted since the original treaty. Some of the most important of these measures are

- The Convention for the Conservation of Antarctic Seals (1972): Allows only limited seal hunting in the waters south of 60°S. The objective is to promote and achieve the protection, scientific study, and rational use of Antarctic seals and to maintain a satisfactory balance within the ecological system of Antarctica.
- The Convention on the Conservation of Antarctic Marine Living Resources (1980): Governs all harvesting and research activities involving living resources. Its objective is to safeguard the environment and protect the integrity of the ecosystem of the seas surrounding Antarctica and to conserve Antarctic marine living resources.
- Convention on the Regulation of Antarctic Mineral Resource Activities (1988): Regulates activities that seek to exploit Antarctic mineral resources in an effort to prohibit activities that would cause damage to the environment or ecosystems of the Antarctic or affect global or regional climate patterns.
- The Protocol on Environmental Protection to the Antarctic Treaty (1991): Provides comprehensive protection for the Antarctic environment through five annexes on marine pollution, flora and fauna, environmental impact assessments, waste management, and protected areas.

As mentioned in Chapter 13, in 1994 the International Whaling Commission (IWC) set up the Southern Ocean Sanctuary for whales.

The sanctuary protects the majority of the Southern Ocean south of 40°S, where threatened fin and humpback whales and several other species spend much of their year.

Some nations have passed their own laws governing behavior in the Antarctic. The Antarctic Conservation Act is a federal law, enacted in the United States in 1978, that protects native mammals, birds, plants, and their ecosystems. The law applies to all U.S. citizens and to all expeditions to Antarctica that originate from the United States.

Unless authorized by permit, the act makes it unlawful to

- take native mammals or birds
- engage in harmful interference
- enter specially designated areas
- introduce species to Antarctica
- introduce substances designated as pollutants
- discharge designated pollutants
- import certain Antarctic items into the United States.

PROTECTIONS GOVERNING THE ARCTIC

The very different history and geography of the Arctic has resulted in a different approach to environmental protection than the arrangements set up for the Antarctic. People have lived in the Arctic for thousands of years, and many nations now share the region. All of these people have a long history of utilizing the Arctic's resources. As a result of this multifaceted history, the protections that govern the Arctic are generally a hodge-podge of laws that are used by individual nations to regulate their own lands and waters.

The first coordinated effort at environmental protection in the Arctic took place in 1991 when eight Arctic nations signed the Arctic Environmental Protection Strategy (AEPS). The Arctic Council, an international organization consisting of governments and indigenous communities that share the Arctic region, was formed in 1996 by the Ottawa Declaration. The objective of the Arctic Council is to ensure that the environmental, social, and economic developments of the region adhere to sustainable practices. The nations that are currently members include Canada, Denmark, Finland, Iceland, Norway, Russia, Sweden, and the United States. The indigenous communities that are permanent participants of the council are the Aleut International Association, the Arctic Athabaskan Council, the Gwinch'in Council International, the Inuit Circumpolar Conference, the Russian Association of Indigenous Peoples of the North, and the Saami Council.

There are five working groups within the Arctic Council:

- The Arctic Monitoring and Assessment Program (AMAP) provides reliable and sufficient information on the status of, and threats to, the Arctic environment. AMAP also provides scientific advice to support Arctic governments in controlling and remedying damage from contaminants.
- Conservation of Arctic Flora and Fauna (CAFF) promotes the conservation of biodiversity and the sustainable use of living resources. CAFF monitors biodiversity, fully utilizing traditional knowledge, to detect the impacts of global climate change. CAFF advises Arctic communities on how to respond to these impacts.
- Protection of the Arctic Marine Environment (PAME) is leading the development of an Arctic Marine Strategic Plan (AMSP), which will guide the Arctic Council in its efforts to protect Arctic seas.
- Through the Sustainable Development Working Group, the Arctic states have declared their commitment to improving human conditions in the Arctic, including such health issues as the relationship between pollution and health.
- The Emergency Preparedness Prevention and Response (EPPR) Working Group exchanges information on the best practices for preventing oil spills and preparing to respond to spills should they occur, as well as practical response measures for use in the event of a spill.

The Arctic Council has two special initiatives. The first, the Arctic Council Plan to Eliminate Pollution in the Arctic (ACAP), addresses the pollution sources identified by AMAP and works to reduce Arctic pollution, including the cleaner production and control of PCBs, obsolete pesticides, dioxins, and, more recently, new chemical pollutants. The second special initiative is to coordinate the work of 300 scientists to produce the Arctic Climate Impact Assessment (ACIA), which evaluates Arctic climate change and predicts its future consequences to ecosystems, animals, and people. Some of the results of the report are presented in Chapters 6, 7, and 8.

INDIVIDUAL CONTRIBUTIONS TO PROTECTING THE POLAR REGIONS

Many of the environmental problems in the polar regions are the result of the lifestyles and behaviors of the people who live in lower latitude nations. So it follows that any contributions that people around the world make to reduce their environmental impact can help to preserve the fragile polar environment and ecosystems. Making wise transportation choices, reducing the consumption of manufactured products, and encouraging political leaders to promote sound environmental policies are some ways that an individual can positively affect the polar environment.

Perhaps most important is for people to reduce the amount of energy they use since fossil-fuel burning emits greenhouse gases and other pollutants. Most energy consumption is involved with transportation and every gallon of gasoline burned emits 20 pounds (9 kg) of CO_2 and other pollutants. Walking, taking public transportation, or driving an energy-efficient vehicle can reduce or eliminate an individual's negative environmental impact from transportation. Being energy efficient by turning off electrical appliances and unplugging electronics when they are not in use can save energy, as can keeping the thermostat set to a reasonable temperature, using a clothesline instead of a clothes dryer, and using compact fluorescent light bulbs.

The Environmental Protection Agency (EPA) uses their Energy Star label to certify major appliances that meet higher standards of energy efficiency. Since manufacturing uses a great deal of energy, purchasing recycled products, or avoiding purchases entirely, uses less or no energy. Fossil fuels are also used in creating plastics, so simple efforts like taking a canvas bag to the supermarket and drinking water in a reusable bottle will help.

Reducing consumption also lessens chemical pollution. Limited use of chemical pesticides, insecticides, artificial fertilizers, and other harmful chemicals is recommended. Additionally, by reducing consumption, fewer materials will need to be mined, manufactured, transported, and disposed of, all of which can reduce a person's pollution impact. When it is necessary to dispose of hazardous waste, people should use the methods recommended by the local sanitation department.

By being politically active, an individual can encourage the government to develop policies that promote energy conservation, energy efficiency, sound manufacturing and waste disposal practices, and that provide funds for the research and development of energy-efficient technologies. Adults can vote for local, state, and national leaders who encourage environmentally sound policies. Political leaders can also be encouraged to see that the United States participates in international treaties that seek to limit pollution emissions and that protect the polar regions.

WRAP-UP

Although the polar regions are not too remote for the spread of environmental problems, they are, in many ways, too remote for widespread environmental protections. The regions are not as well known as many places where the population density is higher, so the problems are not as well understood. They are also more difficult to regulate because of the difficulty in policing such large areas. Protections in the Antarctic are far-reaching because the area is preserved for scientific purposes and is saved from most other pursuits. Protections in the Arctic are difficult to enact because they involve many nations with different goals. Nonetheless, the Arctic Council is working to ensure that the region is developed sustainably and that the needs of the environment and of the indigenous people are taken into account.

Conclusion

The polar regions are remote, unique, and largely unfamiliar. What they are not is pristine—at least, not as pristine as most people imagine them to be. While these areas do not generate much pollution themselves, they seem to acquire a great deal of pollution from the rest of the world. Environmental problems that affect the entire planet are sometimes even more concentrated in the polar regions, due to the motions of air and water and the environmental conditions found near the poles. One example is ozone depletion, which, due to atmospheric circulation and the frigid temperatures of the south polar area, is magnified enough to produce the Antarctic ozone hole. At the north polar region, pollutants travel by air, ocean currents, and river water to the Arctic Ocean, where they tend to either stagnate or become absorbed into the food chain. Once in the marine food web, their impacts magnify so that some top predators, including the native people, have become highly contaminated.

Polar bears have come to symbolize the problems facing the Arctic region. The image most people have of these animals no longer melds with the reality. Polar bears are thought to live in remote places and hunt seals from sea ice in a cold and unspoiled environment. However, for a variety of reasons, polar bears are suffering from environmental ills more than most organisms that live much closer to human development. As top predators within the marine food web, polar bears accumulate enormous amounts of toxic chemicals in their body fat over the course of their lives. The bears reach sexual maturity late, they give birth to few young over many years, and the mothers nurse their young for long periods, so they have ample time to accumulate chemicals and pass them on to their offspring. Due to warming temperatures, the sea ice that the bears depend on for hunting platforms lasts for a shorter period of time during the winter, and emaciated bears are now being observed more frequently. Polar bears have been seen drowning as they try to swim between ice floes that are now drifting too far apart. While polar bears are still hunted, an even greater threat to them may be the excess harvesting of their food sources.

The Antarctic suffers from a different set of environmental problems. Antarctic animals have contaminants in their bodies, but levels are low when compared to the organisms of the Arctic. A greater problem is the Antarctic ozone hole, which allows more ultraviolet light to strike the region and damage plankton and other Southern Ocean organisms. Overhunting has been an enormous problem, as whaling and sealing took countless animals in the past—so many that some populations have not yet recovered. Other marine mammal populations are suffering from problems due to their reduced numbers. Overfishing contributes to the imbalance of the Antarctic ecosystem because fish are also the food source for many other Antarctic organisms. Krill are even more important, and their populations have declined precipitously in recent decades due to a combination of increased ultraviolet radiation, warmer ocean temperatures, and overfishing. Populations of some penguins have been reduced due to a decline in their prey and to the effects of global warming that interfere with their habits. For example, when icebergs created by global warming block the ability of a parent bird to get to the sea, the parent and its chick are unlikely to survive.

With no native people inhabiting it, the Antarctic does not have the historic record of observation and study that the Arctic has. The Inuit people of the Arctic are keen observers of their environment because their survival strategy depends entirely on understanding conditions so that they can hunt and fish safely and successfully. The Inuit have traditionally hunted and fished from sea ice, tracked migrating herds of animals across the frozen tundra, and built homes from ice and snow. Although most of the Inuit have taken on some modern ways, such as using modern machines for transportation and hunting, they are becoming less able to live as they once did as snow, ice, and permafrost melt away. Like other top Arctic predators, the Inuit also have high concentrations of toxic chemicals in their bodies. They are now advised not to eat as many of their traditional foods for their own health and so that they do not pass too high a level of chemical contaminants on to their children.

The Inuit are extremely important because they are the only voice the polar regions have. They have witnessed the changes to their environment, particularly those caused by warmer temperatures, and they are fighting to save it. By petitioning the Inter-American Commission on Human Rights, they are drawing global attention to global warming as a human rights issue. They say that they will not be able to live traditional lives in their traditional homeland if temperatures continue to warm too much. Whether something will come of their efforts while there is still time to preserve the Arctic world that their ancestors knew, remains to be seen.

There is another side to this issue that involves all people of the Arctic nations. Entrepreneurs have noted that the loss of ice will allow people unprecedented access to the natural resources of the area. Estimates by the United States Geological Survey suggest that as much as one-quarter of the world's unknown oil deposits are beneath the Arctic Ocean. The United Nations Environment Programme (UNEP) estimates that while 15% of the Arctic was affected by oil and gas exploration, mining, ports, and other industries in 2000, by 2050 80% will be affected. Clearer seas will open up shipping lanes and cut thousands of miles off of the routes that are currently used. Even the Inuit will gain economically as more jobs in the energy and other industries become available.

The irony is that the oil and gas that will be developed due to a warmer Arctic will create additional greenhouse gas emissions, which will further exacerbate global warming. There are other problems as well: The more oil that is drilled and transported, particularly in the treacherous, iceberg-laden waters of the far north, the more likely it is that there will be a spill. Tankers, still mostly single-hulled, are particularly at risk of being punctured by icebergs. If—or, more likely, when—a spill does occur, the oil will not break up quickly, because the chemical and biological activity that breaks down oil happens more slowly at colder temperatures. Furthermore, ice keeps wave action from breaking up the oil. Russia is a major player in Arctic oil development, but the country does not have a good history of environmental protection, nor does it have the resources to combat a spill, should one occur. Development of oil fields also brings pollution, roads, and more development.

As remote as the polar regions are, it is now clear to scientists that they are greatly affected by human activities that take place in the rest of the world. This fact should be a call for people in the lower latitudes to be conscious of the far-reaching effects of their actions. These concerns start with the polar regions, but they do not end there. As the polar regions—the proverbial "canary in the coal mine"—change, so does the rest of the Earth.

Glossary

acidification The alteration of seawater so that it becomes more acidic due to increased atmospheric carbon dioxide that ends up in the ocean and creates carbonic acid.

adaptation A structure or behavior alteration that is inheritable, that is, able to be passed from one generation to the next.

aerosols Solid or liquid pollutants that are small enough to stay suspended in the air. They are generally nontoxic but can seriously reduce visibility.

air pollution Contamination of the air by particulates and toxic gases in concentrations that can endanger human and environmental health. Also known as smog.

albedo The amount of light that reflects back off a surface; snow and ice have high albedo, mud has low albedo.

algae Algae are a very diverse group that make up a portion of two different kingdoms; they are not plants, although some look like plants and all photosynthesize. Most are aquatic; most seaweeds are algae.

alien species Also called invasive species; organisms that are introduced by human activities into a location where they are not native; marine invasive species often travel in the ballast water of ships.

androgens Male vertebrate sex hormones that develop and regulate the functioning of the sex organs.

Antarctic The territory between the Antarctic Circle, at 66° 33' 38" S, and the South Pole; the Antarctic is sometimes defined as the territory lying south of the tree line in the Southern Hemisphere.

Antarctic Circumpolar Current   The ocean current that flows between the tips of the southern continents and Antarctica; the Antarctic Circumpolar Current is fast and large, effectively separating Antarctica from the world's oceans.

aquaculture   The raising and harvesting of aquatic plants, fish, and shellfish in a water environment under controlled conditions.

Arctic   The territory between the Arctic Circle, at 66° 33' 38" N, and the North Pole; the Arctic is sometimes defined as the territory lying north of the tree line in the Northern Hemisphere.

Arctic haze   Pollutants that are brought by atmospheric currents into the Arctic and form a dense layer of air pollution during the winter.

atmosphere   The gases surrounding a planet or moon.

aurora   A display of lights of many colors caused by the collision of electrically charged particles from the solar wind with gases in the atmosphere. In the Northern Hemisphere, the phenomenon is known as the *aurora borealis* or northern lights; in the Southern Hemisphere it is known as the *aurora australis* or southern lights.

baleen whales   These whales use the stiff, fibrous baleen in their mouths to filter krill and other small creatures out of seawater; the group includes the largest animals that have ever lived, blue whales.

benthic   Organisms that live on the sea bottom.

bioaccumulation   The accumulation of toxic substances within living organisms.

biodegradable   Word used to describe waste that living organisms can decompose into harmless inorganic materials.

biodiversity   The number of species in a given habitat.

biomarker   A characteristic that is objectively measured that can indicate the presence of a toxic chemical, for example.

biomass   The mass of all the living matter in a given area or volume of a habitat.

biome   All of the ecosystems with similar climate and life around the world; examples of some biomes include tundra, tropical rain forest, and desert.

boreal forest   Frigid biome of northern Eurasia and Canada, dominated by fir trees and diverse mammal life; snow is the dominant precipitation.

bycatch   Fish that are unwanted by fishers because they are too small or too low in value, or that a fisher is not licensed to catch. About 25% of all marine creatures caught are bycatch.

cancer   A group of more than 100 distinct diseases that are typified by the uncontrolled growth of abnormal cells in the body.

carbon dioxide (CO_2)   A molecule made of one carbon and two oxygen atoms that is an important component of the atmosphere and an extremely effective greenhouse gas.

carbon economy   The current economic structure, which relies on the use of carbon-based fuels, primarily fossil fuels.

carbon sequestration   Storage of carbon in one reservoir so that it is no longer part of the carbon cycle; two natural reservoirs for carbon sequestration are forests and oceans.

carbon tax   A tax placed on energy sources that emit carbon dioxide into the atmosphere to better pay for the costs of fossil fuel burning; the tax is intended to inspire conservation and research and development of non carbon based technologies.

carcinogen   A substance that causes cancer. Carcinogens affect people who have a genetic predisposition for getting the disease more than those who do not, except in cases of extreme exposure to the carcinogen.

carnivore   An animal that eats other animals.

cetaceans   Marine mammals that include whales, dolphins, and porpoises.

chlorofluorocarbon (CFC)   An anthropogenic gas that rises into the stratosphere and breaks down ozone.

chlorophyll   The molecule that gives plants their green color and allows them to carry on photosynthesis.

climate model   A construction of climate using available data and an understanding of the interactions of the atmosphere, hydrosphere, and biosphere; climate models can be used to predict future climate.

consumer   An organism that feeds on other plants or animals for food energy.

convection cell   A current in which warm material rises, then moves sideways and cools. When it becomes dense enough, it sinks. It then moves back to where it began and starts the process over.

crustaceans   Mostly marine members of the phylum Arthropoda; crustaceans include lobsters, crabs, and shrimp.

decomposer   An organism that breaks down the body parts of dead organisms or their waste into nutrients that can be used by other plants and animals.

deoxyribonucleic acid (DNA)   The nucleic acid that carries hereditary information from parent cell to daughter cell. When a cell divides, its DNA makes an identical copy of itself that is passed to its daughter.

Dichlorodiphenyltrichloroethane (DDT)   This toxic chemical was a very effective insecticide but was withdrawn from production when its negative effects (and those of its breakdown products) on birds and mammals were realized.

dioxins   Toxic chemicals that are byproducts of the manufacture of other chemicals and have been shown to be hazardous to animals and possibly humans.

ecosystem   The interrelationships of the plants and animals of a region and the raw materials that they need to live.

electron   A negatively charged particle that orbits an atom's nucleus.

El Niño   A temporary warming of the Pacific Ocean that has implications for global weather patterns.

endangered species   An organism that is threatened with extinction.

Endangered Species Act of 1973   A U.S. law that protects all animal and plant life threatened with extinction, including threatened species, defined as those that are likely to become endangered in the foreseeable future.

endemic species   A species that is found only in a particular location, such as on an island.

endocrine disruptor   A compound that interrupts the functions of the endocrine system, often interfering with the sexual development or success of a species; most are estrogens or estrogen mimics.

endocrine system   The system of the body that controls the internal environment by sending out hormones as chemical messengers.

equinox   Each of two days of the year when the Sun is directly over the Equator; In the Northern Hemisphere, vernal (spring) equinox falls on March 21 or 22, and autumnal (fall) equinox falls on September 21 or 22.

erosion   The movement of sediments from one location to another by water, wind, ice, or gravity.

estrogens   Female vertebrate sex hormones that trigger the development of the sex organs and control the reproductive cycle.

evaporation   The change of state of a substance from a liquid to a gas, such as the change from liquid water to water vapor.

evolution   Change through time. In science, evolution usually refers to organic evolution, which is the change in organisms through time by the process of natural selection.

extinct   A species becomes extinct if no member survives and reproduces. This can occur in two ways: First, the species cannot evolve to keep up with a changing environment; it dies out and its genes are lost. Second, the species evolves into another species and its most useful genes are preserved.

fishery   A species of fish in a particular region, such as the Arctic cod fishery; usually the term is used to describe fish populations that can be fished commercially.

food chain A chain that tracks food energy as it moves from producer to primary consumer to secondary consumer and so on, ending with decomposers.

food web Overlapping food chains that form a web that makes up the biological portion of an ecosystem.

fossil fuels Ancient plants that have decayed and been transformed into useable fuel, especially coal and petroleum. These fuels are actually stored ancient sunshine.

gene The unit of inheritance that passes a trait from one generation to the next.

glacier A moving mass of ice and snow that forms on land. Glaciers grow when the amount of snow falling in winter exceeds the amount that melts in spring and summer; they shrink when annual snowmelt exceeds annual snowfall.

global warming The worldwide rising of average global temperature; usually refers to the temperature increases that have taken place in the past one-and-a-half centuries.

greenhouse effect The trapping of heat that radiates from the Earth. Without it, Earth's average temperature would be much lower.

greenhouse gas A gas that absorbs heat radiated from the Earth. Greenhouse gases include carbon dioxide, methane, ozone, nitrous oxide, and chlorofluorocarbons.

gyre Five large ocean currents that travel in circles around major portions of the ocean basins; they rotate clockwise in the Northern Hemisphere and counterclockwise in the Southern Hemisphere.

habitat The environment in which an organism lives, including such distinctive features as climate, resource availability, predators, and many others.

heavy metal A metal with high weight, especially one that is toxic to organisms.

hemoglobin The red pigment of red blood cells that carries oxygen to the tissues.

herbivore   Plant-eating animals that make up the second level of a food web (the first level of consumers).

hermaphroditism   A condition in which an organism has both male and female sex organs.

hormones   Chemical messengers sent out by the endocrine glands to regulate body processes such as growth and development.

hydrocarbon   An organic compound composed of hydrogen and carbon; fossil fuels are hydrocarbons.

iceberg   A chunk of ice that breaks off a glacier and floats on the water.

ice cap   A mass of ice that moves outward from a center where it accumulates; currently Earth has two ice caps, in Greenland and Antarctica.

icefish   A group of about 200 species of fish that are endemic to the Antarctic; icefish have amazing adaptations that allow them to live in the frigid water, including blood that practically consists of ice water.

ice sheet   An enormous glacier that covers a land surface greater than 19,305 square miles (50,000 sq. km) in area; the only two ice sheets currently on Earth are the Greenland in the Arctic and the much larger Antarctic ice sheet on the Antarctic continent.

ice shelf   A floating sheet of water that projects off a glacier or ice sheet onto coastal waters.

indigenous   Originating in, and characteristic of, a particular region or country; native to its area.

Inuit   The native people who have lived in the Arctic region for thousands of years; their traditional way of life was extremely well adapted to the harsh polar environment.

invasive species   Also called alien species; organisms that are introduced by human activities into a location where they are not native; marine invasive species often travel in the ballast water of ships.

invertebrate   An animal without a backbone.

inversion An increase in atmospheric air temperature in the atmosphere with height—the opposite of normal conditions.

keystone species A species of plant or animal that is crucial to the health of the entire community; often a top carnivore.

krill Crustacean zooplankton that make up the greatest biomass of any multicellular creature on Earth; an important part of the diet of many marine organisms, particularly in the Antarctic.

Kyoto Protocol International treaty that went into force in 2004 in which 36 industrialized nations agreed to cut back their CO_2 emissions to at least 5% below 1990 levels by 2012.

latitude The angular distance of any point on the surface of the Earth north or south of the equator.

lead A metal that once was added to gasoline, paint, pipes, and other materials; it is toxic even in tiny doses.

Marine Mammals Protection Act, 1972 A United States law that bans taking (harvesting, hunting, capturing, killing or attempting to kill) or importing any marine mammals or mammal product in United States territorial waters and fisheries.

mercury A heavy metal that is released by burning coal, in municipal and medical wastes, and by volcanic processes.

methane A hydrocarbon gas (CH_4) that is the major component of natural gas. Methane is also a natural component of the atmosphere and a greenhouse gas.

methane hydrate Water molecules in an unstable icy cage that contains a methane molecule and is not held together by chemical bonds; the methane from these hydrates is useable as fuel.

methyl mercury The organic form of mercury; this heavy metal is most toxic in this form.

Montreal Protocol An international agreement that went into force in 1989 to phase out the use of ozone-depleting substances. Full name: The Montreal Protocol on Substances that Deplete the Ozone Layer.

mutation A random change in a gene; it may be beneficial, harmful, or neutral to the success of the individual and species.

myoglobin   A relative of hemoglobin, myoglobin tightly binds oxygen into muscles for their use during exertion.

natural selection   The mechanism that drives organic evolution. Natural processes affect the reproductive success of an organism, which steers the way a species will evolve.

nitrous oxides   NO and NO_2 referred to collectively as NO_x. They are natural components of the atmosphere and act as greenhouse gases.

Northern Hemisphere   The half of the Earth from the Equator to the North Pole.

nutrients   Biologically important elements that are critical to growth or to building shells or bones; nitrates, phosphorous, carbonate, and silicate are some nutrients for marine organisms.

overfishing   The taking of so many fish from a fishery that the fish population cannot replenish itself.

ozone   A molecule composed of three oxygen atoms and symbolized as O_3. Ozone is a pollutant in the lower atmosphere; but in the upper atmosphere, it protects life on the Earth's surface from the Sun's deadly ultraviolet radiation.

ozone hole   A "hole" in the ozone layer where ozone concentrations are diminished; the term usually refers to the Antarctic ozone hole.

ozone layer   The layer found at between 9 and 19 miles (15 and 30 km) in the stratosphere, where ozone is concentrated; this layer shields us from the Sun's ultraviolet radiation.

pack ice   Sea ice joined together to make a large platform.

permafrost   Permanently frozen soil; common in the polar regions.

persistent organic pollutants (POPs)   Chemical substances that persist in the environment, bioaccumulate throughout the food web, and may damage human health and the environment.

photochemical smog   Air pollution that forms when sunlight facilitates the chemical reaction of pollutants such as nitrogen oxides and hydrocarbons.

photosynthesis The process in which plants use carbon dioxide and water to produce sugar and oxygen. The simplified chemical reaction is $6CO_2 + 12H_2O$ + solar energy $= C_6H_{12}O_6 + 6O_2 + 6H_2O$.

phytoplankton Microscopic plantlike, usually single-celled, organisms found at the surface of the ocean; they are the planet's single greatest source of oxygen.

pinnipeds Meat-eating marine mammals that includes seals, sea lions, and walruses.

plankton Tiny plants (phytoplankton) and animals (zooplankton) that live at the sea surface and form the lower levels of the ocean's food web.

plankton bloom An explosion in phytoplankton population due to the addition of a substance that was limited; most commonly, light in polar regions.

Pleistocene Ice Age The most recent ice age in Earth history (also referred to as the Ice Age), from between 1.8 million and 10,000 years before the present. The Pleistocene consists of four glacial and three interglacial periods.

polar stratospheric clouds (PSCs) Stratospheric clouds that are composed of water and nitric acid; they are necessary for the breakdown of chlorofluorocarbons in the atmosphere.

pollutants Artificial impurities that are found in the atmosphere, water, or land. Pollutants include carbon dioxide (CO_2), oil, heavy metals, sewage, fertilizers, toxic chemicals, and invasive species.

polychlorinated bipheyls (PCBs) Extremely stable, water soluble persistent organic pollutants that bioaccumulate and are found globally.

polynuclear aromatic hydrocarbons (PAHs) A weathering product of crude oil that can damage marine life after an oil spill.

predator An organism that kills and eats other animals for food energy.

prey An animal that is eaten by other animals for food energy.

primary producer An organism that produces food energy from inorganic substances; the term usually refers to a plant that photosynthesizes to create food energy.

respiration The process by which an organism exchanges gases with the environment. Note that in the reaction, sugar and CO_2 are converted into oxygen and water with the release of energy: $C_6H_{12}O_6 + 6O_2 = 6CO_2 + 6H_2O$ + released energy.

scavenger An animal that eats dead plants or animals for food energy.

sea ice Frozen seawater; sea ice can be permanent or it can be seasonal, melting in the summer and forming again in the winter.

slash-and-burn agriculture A form of agriculture mostly practiced in the tropics; rain forest plants are slashed down and then burned to clear the land for planting.

Southern Hemisphere The half of the Earth from the Equator to the South Pole.

species A classification of organisms that includes those that can or do interbreed and produce fertile offspring; members of a species share the same gene pool.

stratosphere The upper atmosphere, which rises from the troposphere to about 30 miles (45 km) up. The stratosphere contains the ozone layer.

summer solstice The day of the year, June 21 or 22, when the Sun is farthest north in the sky; this is the longest day of the year in the Northern Hemisphere and the shortest in the Southern Hemisphere.

sustainable A type of resource use that does not compromise the current need for resources or those of future generations for present economic gain.

thermal expansion The addition of heat to a liquid causes molecules to vibrate more vigorously, which increases the distances between them and causes the liquid to expand; as the globe warms, thermal expansion will be a significant cause of sea level rise.

threshold effect A value beyond which an abrupt response is observed; e.g., if enough Arctic ice melts, it leaves behind so much open water that new ice stops forming.

tipping point Regarding climate change, the point of no return as a result of positive feedbacks.

toothed whales Whales with teeth; these whales tend to be smaller than baleen whales, but they are predators, eating seals and fish, among other things.

transboundary pollution Pollution that travels over a political border so that it affects a different nation or region than the one where it was generated; most Arctic pollution is transboundary pollution.

tributyltin (TBT) A tin-containing compound that is an effective anti-fouling agent and an endocrine disruptor.

trophic level The levels of energy within the food web: Primary producers make up the first trophic level; the herbivores that eat the primary producers make up the second; the carnivores that eat the herbivores make up the third; and so on.

troposphere The lowest layer of the Earth's atmosphere, rising from sea level to about 36,000 feet (11 km).

tundra Biome of the polar regions and high altitudes in which low-lying, scrubby plants survive against the frigid cold, wind, and short growing season.

ultraviolet radiation (UV) Shortwave, high-energy solar radiation; the highest energy wavelengths of UV are extremely harmful to life.

upwelling Upward flow of lower density water, often nutrient rich, from the deep ocean to the sea surface.

vascular plant Plants with roots, stems, leaves, vascular tissue for transporting water and food, and a cuticle that helps them resist desiccation.

vertebrate An animal with a backbone; fish, amphibians, reptiles, birds, and mammals are all vertebrates.

water vapor Water (H_2O) in its gaseous state.

wavelength In a wave, the distance from crest to crest or trough to trough.

westerly winds or westerlies Winds that move from west to east between the approximate latitudes 30° to 50° on both the north and south sides of the equator.

wetland   A poorly drained region that is covered all or part of the time with fresh or salt water.

winter solstice   The day of the year, December 21 or 22, when the Sun is farthest south in the sky; this is the longest day of the year in the Southern Hemisphere and the shortest in the Northern Hemisphere.

zooplankton   Tiny marine animals that are unable to swim on their own and drift with the currents.

Further Reading

Berton, Pierre. *The Arctic Grail: The Quest for the Northwest Passage and the North Pole, 1818–1909.* Guilford, Conn.: The Lyons Press, 2000.

Carroll, Sean B. "The Bloodless Fish of Bouvet Island: DNA and Evolution in Action." *Skeptical Inquirer* 30 (Sept.–Oct. 2006): 39–44.

Centre for Atmospheric Science, University of Cambridge. "The Ozone Hole Tour." Available online. http://www.atm.ch.cam.ac.uk/tour/. Accessed November 16, 2006.

Colborn, Theo, Diane Dumanoski, and John Peterson Myers. *Our Stolen Future: Are We Threatening Our Fertility, Intelligence, and Survival?* New York: Plume, 1997.

Cone, Marla. *Silent Snow: The Slow Poisoning of the Arctic.* New York: Grove Press, 2005.

Doran, Peter. "Cold, Hard Facts." *The New York Times*, July 27, 2006.

Fogg, G.E. *A History of Antarctic Science.* New York: Cambridge University Press, 2005.

Gore, Al. *An Inconvenient Truth: The Planetary Emergency of Global Warming and What We Can Do About It.* New York: Rodale, 2006.

Hansen, Jim. "The Threat to the Planet." *New York Review of Books* 53 (July 13, 2006). Available online. http://www.nybooks.com/articles/19131. Accessed September 6, 2006.

Lopez, Barry. *Arctic Dreams: Imagination and Desire in a Northern Landscape.* New York: Charles Scribner's Sons, 1986.

McGonigal, David, and Lynn Woodworth. *Antarctica and the Arctic: The Complete Encyclopedia.* New York: Firefly Books, 2001.

Revkin, Andrew C. *The North Pole Was Here: Puzzles and Perils at the Top of the World.* Boston: Kingfisher, 2006.

Salazar, Jorge. "The North Pole Was Here," Interview with Andrew Revkin, Earth and Sky radio, February 24, 2006.

Web Sites

Alliance to Save Energy
http://www.ase.org/.
Helping people save energy as the quickest, cleanest, and cheapest way to a healthier economy, a cleaner environment, and greater energy security.

The Antarctic Treaty Secretariat
http://www.ats.aq.
The official Web site of the Antarctic Treaty Secretariat.

Arctic Council
http://www.arctic-council.org.
The Web site of the Arctic Council, a forum for cooperation, coordination, and interaction between Arctic states, indigenous communities, and other Arctic residents.

The Arctic Climate Impact Assessment (ACIA)
http://www.acia.uaf.edu/.
The Web site of the group affiliated with the Arctic Monitoring and Assessment Program that assesses climate change in the Arctic; includes links to ACIA reports.

The Arctic Monitoring and Assessment Program (AMAP)
http://amap.no/.
The Web site of the international organization established to implement components of the Arctic Environmental Protection Strategy.

BBC Science & Nature
http://www.bbc.co.uk/sn/.
Science and nature stories, news, and fact files.

Intergovernmental Panel on Climate Change (IPCC)

http://www.ipcc.ch/.

*Access to reports, speeches, graphics, and other materials from
the IPCC.*

International Whaling Commission (IWC)

http://www.iwcoffice.org/index.htm.

*Up-to-date information about whales and whaling from the IWC, which
was established in 1946.*

**National Climatic Data Center, National Oceanic and Atmospheric
Administration (NOAA)**

http://www.ncdc.noaa.gov/oa/ncdc.html.

*The world's largest archive of climate data from land-based, marine,
satellite, and upper air sources, with interpretation and links to
many weather topics.*

Our Stolen Future

http://www.ourstolenfuture.org/.

*Web site tracking recent developments in the field of endocrine disrup-
tion by the authors of the book* Our Stolen Future, *listed above;
includes a list of widespread pesticides with endocrine-disrupting
effects.*

Pew Center on Global Climate Change

http://www.pewclimate.org.

*Climate analysis by business leaders, policy makers, scientists, and
other experts, based on sound science; includes the primer
Climate Change 101.*

RealClimate

http://www.realclimate.org.

*Written by working climate scientists for the public and journalists to
provide content and context for climate change stories.*

Index

About the Author

DANA DESONIE, PH.D., has written about earth, ocean, space, life, and environmental sciences for more than a decade. Her work has appeared in educational lessons, textbooks, and magazines, and on radio and the Web. Her 1996 book, *Cosmic Collisions*, described the importance of asteroids and comets in Earth history and the possible consequences of a future asteroid collision with the planet. Before becoming a science writer, she received a doctorate in oceanography, spending weeks at a time at sea, mostly in the tropics, and one amazing day at the bottom of the Pacific in the research submersible *Alvin*. She now resides in Phoenix, Arizona, with her neuroscientist husband, Miles Orchinik, and their two children.